THE STRIVING TOGETHER STUDY LIBRARY

GALATIANS
NO TURNING BACK

EXPANDED OUTLINES AND COMMENTS BY
PAUL CHAPPELL

Copyright © 2013 by Striving Together Publications. All Scripture quotations are taken from the King James Version.

First published in 2013 by Striving Together Publications, a ministry of Lancaster Baptist Church, Lancaster, CA 93535. Striving Together Publications is committed to providing tried, trusted, and proven books that will further equip local churches to carry out the Great Commission. Your comments and suggestions are valued.

All rights reserved. No part of this book may be reproduced, stored in a retrieval system, or transmitted in any form or by any means—electronic, mechanical, photocopy, recording, or otherwise—without written permission of the publisher, except for brief quotations in printed reviews.

Striving Together Publications
4020 E. Lancaster Blvd.
Lancaster, CA 93535
800.201.7748

Cover design by Jeremy Lofgren
Layout by Craig Parker
Edited by Melodie Workman and Monica Bass
Special thanks to our proofreaders.

The author and publication team have put forth every effort to give proper credit to quotes and thoughts that are not original with the author. It is not our intent to claim originality with any quote or thought that could not readily be tied to an original source.

ISBN 978-1-59894-247-7
Printed in the United States of America

Dedication

To Dr. Bobby Roberson
Thank you for never turning back.

Table of Contents

Acknowledgments VII
Introduction IX

1. Don't Turn Back (Galatians 1:1–5) 1
2. Reminders for the Faith (Galatians 1:6–10) 9
3. Don't Turn Back on God's Revelation (Galatians 1:11–24) . . . 17
4. In Defense of Grace (Galatians 2:1–10) 25
5. Justified by Faith (Galatians 2:11–19) 33
6. Christ Liveth in Me (Galatians 2:20–21) 39
7. Continuing in the Spirit (Galatians 3:1–5) 47
8. The Family of Faith (Galatians 3:6–14) 53
9. The Promise of Faith (Galatians 3:15–25) 61
10. The Family of God (Galatians 3:26–29) 69
11. Children of God through Christ (Galatians 4:1–7) 75
12. Back to the Blessed Place (Galatians 4:8–15) 79
13. Staying on the Right Path (Galatians 4:16–31) 89
14. Until Christ Be Formed in You (Galatians 4:19–20) 99
15. Stand Fast (Galatians 5:1–6) 109
16. Stay in the Race (Galatians 5:6–15) 115
17. Walking in the Spirit (Galatians 5:16–21) 123
18. Walking with Love (Galatians 5:22–23) 129
19. Walking with Joy (Galatians 5:22–23) 139
20. Walking with Peace (Galatians 5:22–23) 145
21. Walking with Longsuffering (Galatians 5:22–23) 153
22. Walking with Gentleness (Galatians 5:22–23) 161
23. Walking with Goodness (Galatians 5:22–23) 167
24. Walking with Faith (Galatians 5:22–23) 173
25. Walking with Meekness (Galatians 5:22–23) 181
26. Walking with Temperance (Galatians 5:22–23) 187
27. A Spiritual Life (Galatians 5:24–26) 195

28.	A Restorative Church (Galatians 6:1)	201
29.	Make Me a Blessing (Galatians 6:2–5)	209
30.	Sowing and Reaping (Galatians 6:6–8)	215
31.	Let Us Not Be Weary (Galatians 6:9–10)	221
32.	Glory in the Cross (Galatians 6:11–15)	229
33.	Paul's Closing (Galatians 6:16–18)	237

Appendix: Additional Resources for Study 243

Acknowledgments

I would like to thank Rick Houk for his help in study. Thank you, Rick, for your thoroughness and faithfulness.

I also wish to thank Melodie Workman and Monica Bass for helping me prepare these notes for publication.

Especially, I wish to thank the Lancaster Baptist Church family for being a people who love God's Word and walk in its truths. It was a delight to prepare these messages for you.

Introduction

For over twenty-seven years as the pastor of Lancaster Baptist Church, I have had the joy of preaching verse by verse through books of the Bible on Sunday and Wednesday evenings. I thank God for a congregation of people who have evidenced a hunger for the preaching of the Word through the years!

The thirty-three lessons in this volume are outlined sermon notes and comments for the entire book of Galatians that flowed from the study and preparation for this sermon series.

This study is entitled *No Turning Back* because we learn through this epistle of the dangers of turning back to flesh-based systems of righteousness while being encouraged to move forward in the grace-based pattern of the Spirit-filled life.

This is not a full commentary on Galatians. Rather, these are expanded outlines with cross references, word studies, illustrations, and comments. I suggest that you use this volume either as a resource for your own sermon preparation or as a personal study guide for your devotional time. It is my prayer that the lessons in this volume will encourage you as you read and study Galatians along with this companion guide.

May God's Spirit use His Word to remind you of the incredible grace we find in Christ, and may He give you the resolve to never turn back.

Sincerely,

Pastor Paul Chappell
Lancaster, CA
November 2013

OUTLINE ONE

Don't Turn Back
Galatians 1:1–5

1 Paul, an apostle, (not of men, neither by man, but by Jesus Christ, and God the Father, who raised him from the dead;)
2 And all the brethren which are with me, unto the churches of Galatia:
3 Grace be to you and peace from God the Father, and from our Lord Jesus Christ,
4 Who gave himself for our sins, that he might deliver us from this present evil world, according to the will of God and our Father:
5 To whom be glory for ever and ever. Amen.

Introduction

The book of Galatians is the first of twelve epistles Paul wrote. As verse 2 tells us, Galatians was written to a group of local churches in the Roman province of Galatia. This is the only epistle where Paul writes to a group of churches: the rest of Paul's epistles were written either to individuals or to a single local church.

Paul writes this epistle with a deep concern for the Galatian believers who were being confused by false teachers and being drawn away from the gospel of grace. The overarching message of the epistle is, "Don't turn back!"

When Satan is unsuccessful in stopping an individual from trusting Christ, he still does all he can do to cause them to turn back. One of his primary methods to fight the message of God is to deny the authority of the one who gave the message. In the case of the churches of Galatia, that meant Satan would undermine the validity of the Apostle Paul and his message of Christ. This was taking place through false teachers who were Jews coming and teaching the churches of Galatia that they had to keep the law to keep their salvation.

Throughout the book of Galatians, Paul emphasizes the pure message of the gospel—that it is by grace and not works—and he exhorts the Galatian believers to hold the truth and rejoice in the grace of God.

We begin our study of this epistle with Paul's opening words to these churches.

I. The Man God Called (v. 1)

As Paul identifies himself as the writer of this epistle, he notes two facets of his relationship to these churches:

A. Paul the Apostle

An apostle is one who is sent with a commission and a witness of the resurrected Christ. The original twelve apostles were called out by Jesus. Paul is considered an apostle because of his calling on the road to Damascus when he saw the resurrected Christ.

ACTS 9:15–16

15 *But the Lord said unto him, Go thy way: for he is a chosen vessel unto me, to bear my name before the Gentiles, and kings, and the children of Israel:*

16 For I will shew him how great things he must suffer for my name's sake.

Note—There is no biblical precedence for the perpetuity of the office of apostle.

B. Paul the Called

1. **Not from men**

   Paul was not self-appointed. He was not appointed by men. He was appointed by God Himself.

   2 TIMOTHY 1:1
   1 Paul, an apostle of Jesus Christ by the will of God, according to the promise of life which is in Christ Jesus,

   Illustration—Pastors and deacons often ordain young men entering the ministry. This ordination is not "the church" calling a man to the ministry. Rather it is simply a recognition of the fact that *God* has already called him.

2. **By Jesus Christ**

   Jesus called Paul on the road to Damascus, and the church at Antioch confirmed Paul's calling.

   ACTS 13:1–2
   1 Now there were in the church that was at Antioch certain prophets and teachers; as Barnabas, and Simeon that was called Niger, and Lucius of Cyrene, and Manaen, which had been brought up with Herod the tetrarch, and Saul.
   2 As they ministered to the Lord, and fasted, the Holy Ghost said, Separate me Barnabas and Saul for the work whereunto I have called them.

   Note—The God who appointed Paul was the same God who resurrected Christ on the third day!

II. The Method God Used (v. 2)

God's primary vehicle for the spread of the gospel is the local church. This was the Apostle Paul's focus in ministry as well. Thus, he addresses this epistle, not directly to the *Christians* of Galatia, but to the *churches* of Galatia.

A. Planting Local Churches

Paul was a missionary, and planting local churches is the primary work of missions. He labored throughout the region of Galatia to plant local churches.

The work of a pastor or missionary in planting and caring for a local church is not easy, and Paul experienced difficulties in his ministry. He listed many of these in 2 Corinthians—the most biographical of all of his epistles.

2 Corinthians 11:23–28

23 *Are they ministers of Christ? (I speak as a fool) I am more; in labours more abundant, in stripes above measure, in prisons more frequent, in deaths oft.*
24 *Of the Jews five times received I forty stripes save one.*
25 *Thrice was I beaten with rods, once was I stoned, thrice I suffered shipwreck, a night and a day I have been in the deep;*
26 *In journeyings often, in perils of waters, in perils of robbers, in perils by mine own countrymen, in perils by the heathen, in perils in the city, in perils in the wilderness, in perils in the sea, in perils among false brethren;*
27 *In weariness and painfulness, in watchings often, in hunger and thirst, in fastings often, in cold and nakedness.*
28 *Beside those things that are without, that which cometh upon me daily, the care of all the churches.*

Paul cared for churches all over the region:
- Cyprus
- Perga
- Antioch of Pisidia: chief military town

- Iconium: town of pleasure-seeking Greeks
- Lystra: superstitious town at first embraced and then stoned the Apostle
- Derbe

B. Preparing Local Churches

Throughout Paul's ministry, he was heavily invested in caring for the churches God had used him to plant. He visited them, wrote to them, prayed for them, and continued to train church leaders. The purpose of this epistle is to prepare and warn local churches.

Throughout the New Testament, we see Paul used God's Word and loving warnings to prepare local churches.

1. **His Word**

   2 TIMOTHY 2:2

   2 *And the things that thou hast heard of me among many witnesses, the same commit thou to faithful men, who shall be able to teach others also.*

2. **His warnings**

   ACTS 20:29–30

   29 *For I know this, that after my departing shall grievous wolves enter in among you, not sparing the flock.*

   30 *Also of your own selves shall men arise, speaking perverse things, to draw away disciples after them.*

III. The Message God Sent (vv. 3–4)

What was the message God used Paul to send to the spiritually struggling churches of Galatia? Was it a rebuke, a condemnation? No, it was an expression of grace and peace and an exhortation to enjoy their freedom.

A. A Message of Grace (v. 3)

1. **Our position in Christ**

   EPHESIANS 1:6–7

   > 6 To the praise of the glory of his grace, wherein he hath made us accepted in the beloved.
   > 7 In whom we have redemption through his blood, the forgiveness of sins, according to the riches of his grace;

   God's grace extends to people of means as well as people with very little. A child may receive God's grace as well as an elderly person. At the marriage supper of the Lamb, people of every race, age, and social status will sit down together because of the unprejudiced grace of God.

2. **Our disposition toward believers**

   Because of our position in Christ through His grace, our disposition toward other believers should also be one of grace.

   EPHESIANS 4:29

   > 29 Let no corrupt communication proceed out of your mouth, but that which is good to the use of edifying, that it may minister grace unto the hearers.

B. A Message of Peace (v. 3)

The result of God's grace is peace with God.

ROMANS 5:1–2

> 1 Therefore being justified by faith, we have peace with God through our Lord Jesus Christ:
> 2 By whom also we have access by faith into this grace wherein we stand, and rejoice in hope of the glory of God.

C. A Message of Deliverance (v. 4)

The grace and peace of God are through Jesus Christ. God provides every man, woman, boy, and girl with deliverance from sin through the sacrifice of Jesus.

1. **Jesus gave Himself.**
   Jesus became our sin offering.

   GALATIANS 3:13
   13 Christ hath redeemed us from the curse of the law, being made a curse for us: for it is written, Cursed is every one that hangeth on a tree:

2. **Jesus delivers those who trust in Him.**
   Salvation is not earned; it is received. Christ paid the payment for sin. The lost must simply receive His free gift.

   1 PETER 2:24–25
   24 Who his own self bare our sins in his own body on the tree, that we, being dead to sins, should live unto righteousness: by whose stripes ye were healed.
   25 For ye were as sheep going astray; but are now returned unto the Shepherd and Bishop of your souls.

   As a shepherd leaves his fold to rescue a lost sheep, so Jesus came to rescue sinners.

Conclusion (v. 5)

Verse 5 of this passage is a doxology fitting the one who saved us.

A similar passage of praise is found in 1 Timothy:

1 TIMOTHY 1:17
17 Now unto the King eternal, immortal, invisible, the only wise God, be honour and glory for ever and ever. Amen.

Amen, closing both Galatians 1:5 and 1 Timothy 1:17, is a word of affirmation. At the end of this passage, the Apostle Paul reaffirms that what he just said about the glory due to the one who has delivered us is good and true.

OUTLINE TWO

REMINDERS FOR THE FAITH
GALATIANS 1:6–10

6 *I marvel that ye are so soon removed from him that called you into the grace of Christ unto another gospel:*
7 *Which is not another; but there be some that trouble you, and would pervert the gospel of Christ.*
8 *But though we, or an angel from heaven, preach any other gospel unto you than that which we have preached unto you, let him be accursed.*
9 *As we said before, so say I now again, If any man preach any other gospel unto you than that ye have received, let him be accursed.*
10 *For do I now persuade men, or God? or do I seek to please men? for if I yet pleased men, I should not be the servant of Christ.*

Introduction

The reminders in these verses are parallel to a warning Paul also gave to the Corinthian Christians.

1 Corinthians 10:12
12 *Wherefore let him that thinketh he standeth take heed lest he fall.*

These Galatian Christians, once settled in the gospel of grace, were now floundering in their understanding.

I. The Removal from the Faith (v. 6)

A. *The Surprise of the Removal*

The words *I marvel* come from the Greek word *thaumazo*, meaning "to wonder, wonder at, marvel." This verb is in the present tense indicating that Paul may have just heard about it and even as he writes is still amazed by the Galatians' sudden change of direction. Paul had not been departed from these young churches very long when this news came to him.

The word *marvel* is not an angry term but a term of shock. Paul was in shock that even though he had not been gone long, the Galatians had already been swayed in their faith.

B. *The Suddenness of Removal*

In Greek, the phrase *that ye are so soon removed* is *metatithemi*, meaning "to transpose (two things, one of which is put in place of the other), to transfer; to change; to fall away or desert from one person or thing to another."

The Galatian church had transferred their allegiance from Christ to another gospel. They did not lose their salvation, but by following false teachers they would lose their fellowship with God.

1. From Him (God) that called you
God had called the Galatians by His grace.

Ephesians 2:8–9

8 For by grace are ye saved through faith; and that not of yourselves: it is the gift of God:

9 Not of works, lest any man should boast.

2. **To another gospel**
   This gospel was a false gospel that apparently was not based on the grace of God. It may have been one mixed with Jewish tradition, requiring those who followed it to add to grace their works to merit salvation.

II. The Reminder Concerning Faith (vv. 6b–9)

A. *There Are Perverted Gospels (v. 7)*
1. **Another gospel**
   "Another gospel" is not a different *true* gospel, for there is only one true gospel. "Another gospel" meant there were those trying to teach something different than what Paul had taught the Galatians.

   After Paul had preached the true gospel of grace to the Galatia region and many received the gospel unto salvation, somebody preached something else to them and called it "the gospel." But it was a perversion of the true gospel.

   Illustration—The Mormon religion calls their doctrine "another gospel." Scripture is clear that there can be no other true gospel than that which is found in the New Testament—by grace through faith in the finished work of Jesus Christ.

   These false teachers who came to the Galatians were called Judaizers because they attempted to add Jewish ceremonial requirements to the gospel. (We call this *legalism* today. Legalism is any attempt to mix the law and grace.) The Judaizers were dangerous because they called their message a gospel. Their "gospel" taught that to gain entrance into heaven, people must fulfill the law.

   Astringently fulfilling the law nullifies the teaching of grace. In fact, Paul explains later in this same book that there is but one purpose for the law: to help people see their need for Christ's grace.

GALATIANS 3:24

24 *Wherefore the law was our schoolmaster to bring us unto Christ, that we might be justified by faith.*

2. **Troubling Teachers**

The word *trouble* means "to disturb, to agitate."

Paul now reminds these churches that there are those whose purpose is to pervert God's gospel and they "trouble you." This warning against false teachers is given several times throughout the New Testament.

2 TIMOTHY 4:3–4

3 *For the time will come when they will not endure sound doctrine; but after their own lusts shall they heap to themselves teachers, having itching ears;*

4 *And they shall turn away their ears from the truth, and shall be turned unto fables.*

1 JOHN 2:18–19

18 *Little children, it is the last time: and as ye have heard that antichrist shall come, even now are there many antichrists; whereby we know that it is the last time.*

19 *They went out from us, but they were not of us; for if they had been of us, they would no doubt have continued with us: but they went out, that they might be made manifest that they were not all of us.*

B. **There Is A Proven Gospel (vv. 8–9).**
   1. **The meaning of the gospel**

   The word *gospel* means "glad tidings or good news." There are many circumstances, events, and blessings that can bring good news or glad tidings; but there is only

one gospel of grace unto salvation. This is the gospel preached in Acts 13:38–39.

Acts 13:38–39

38 *Be it known unto you therefore, men and brethren, that through this man is preached unto you the forgiveness of sins:*

39 *And by him all that believe are justified from all things, from which ye could not be justified by the law of Moses.*

Galatians 2:15–16

15 *We who are Jews by nature, and not sinners of the Gentiles,*

16 *Knowing that a man is not justified by the works of the law, but by the faith of Jesus Christ, even we have believed in Jesus Christ, that we might be justified by the faith of Christ, and not by the works of the law: for by the works of the law shall no flesh be justified.*

Illustration—D. L. Moody once said, "The thief had nails through both hands, so that he could not work; and a nail through each foot, so that he could not run errands for the Lord; he could not lift a hand or a foot toward his salvation, and yet Christ offered him the gift of God; and he took it. Christ threw him a passport, and took him into Paradise."

2. **The misuse of the gospel (v. 9)**

    The phrase *but though* in verse 8 expresses a conditional statement. In other words, "If we (Paul and those others with him) or an angel from heaven, preach any other gospel unto you than that which we have preached…."

    The word *but* is translated from the Greek conjunction *alla*. This conjunction is the strongest term used in the Greek to show contrast.

Paul explains his words, "though we or an angel from heaven," in 2 Corinthians 11:13–14.

2 CORINTHIANS 11:13–14
13 For such are false apostles, deceitful workers, transforming themselves into the apostles of Christ.
14 And no marvel; for Satan himself is transformed into an angel of light.

In verse 9, Paul repeats this same statement, "If any man preach any other gospel unto you than that ye have received." This repetition adds emphasis to an already serious passage.

The word *accursed* in Greek is *anathema*, meaning "a thing devoted to God without hope of being redeemed, therefore a person or thing doomed to destruction." The Apostle Paul's grave warning to anyone who changes the true message of Christ is that he will be destroyed.

III. The Realization Surrounding Faith (v. 10)

A. *The Cause of the True Faith (v. 10a)*
1. **God's favor**

    The word *persuade*, translated from the Greek word *peitho*, means "to make friends of, to win one's favor, gain one's good will, or to seek to win one, strive to please one."

    Paul asks the Galatian believers here if his goal is to persuade men or God. He uses rhetorical questions to demonstrate that his goal is to persuade or gain the Lord's favor.

    Paul also uses the word *now*, perhaps referring to his past before his salvation. In Paul's religious life before his conversion, he was concerned only with finding favor with man. He explains this in Galatians 1:13–14.

GALATIANS 1:13–14

13 *For ye have heard of my conversation in time past in the Jews' religion, how that beyond measure I persecuted the church of God, and wasted it:*

14 *And profited in the Jews' religion above many my equals in mine own nation, being more exceedingly zealous of the traditions of my fathers.*

Before his conversion, Paul was motivated by pleasing man, but he emphasizes in this passage that "now" his motivation is wholly to please God.

2. **The pleasure of God**

The word *please*, translated from the Greek word *aresko*, means "to please; to strive to please; to accommodate one's self to the opinions, desires, and interests of others." Paul states the obvious: his life is focused on one thing—pleasing Christ. This mission statement meant keeping the gospel Christ-centered, not man-centered.

The Christ-centered gospel taught by Paul was salvation by grace through faith alone. However, a man-centered gospel was what the Jews were trying to get the Gentile churches (like the Galatian church) to believe. This man-centered gospel taught that man has to do his part to earn or to keep his salvation.

Paul's goal was not to please man but to please God. His concern as a soldier of Christ was to please the one who had chosen him to be a soldier in the first place.

2 TIMOTHY 2:4

4 *No man that warreth entangleth himself with the affairs of this life; that he may please him who hath chosen him to be a soldier.*

B. The Commitment of True Faith (v. 10b)

Paul expresses that "to be the servant of Christ," he must forsake being the servant of anyone else. His commitment to Christ would be in question if he called himself a servant of man.

The word *yet* refers to Paul's past compared with his current commitment. If he were still living the way he did before his salvation, then he would be a man-pleaser. If he is a man-pleaser, he is not a servant of Christ. It is obvious that Paul is pledging his allegiance as a servant of Christ.

In 2 Corinthians 12:19, Paul explains that even his preaching and teaching were not meant to please man but to speak before God.

2 Corinthians 12:19

19 *Again, think ye that we excuse ourselves unto you? we speak before God in Christ: but we do all things, dearly beloved, for your edifying.*

Conclusion

Paul's reminder of commitment to God instead of man echoes the conclusion of Jesus' parable in Matthew 25:21.

Matthew 25:21

21 *His lord said unto him, Well done, thou good and faithful servant: thou hast been faithful over a few things, I will make thee ruler over many things: enter thou into the joy of thy lord.*

While living as a servant of Christ may mean sacrifice of earthly friendships, honor, and even sometimes wealth, a committed believer understands that the wealth he seeks lies in Heaven. The honor he desires rests on the lips of his Saviour. And the friendship he knows is one that brings peace that the world cannot give.

OUTLINE THREE

Don't Turn Back on God's Revelation
Galatians 1:11–24

11 But I certify you, brethren, that the gospel which was preached of me is not after man.
12 For I neither received it of man, neither was I taught it, but by the revelation of Jesus Christ.
13 For ye have heard of my conversation in time past in the Jews' religion, how that beyond measure I persecuted the church of God, and wasted it:
14 And profited in the Jews' religion above many my equals in mine own nation, being more exceedingly zealous of the traditions of my fathers.
15 But when it pleased God, who separated me from my mother's womb, and called me by his grace,
16 To reveal his Son in me, that I might preach him among the heathen; immediately I conferred not with flesh and blood:
17 Neither went I up to Jerusalem to them which were apostles before me; but I went into Arabia, and returned again unto Damascus.
18 Then after three years I went up to Jerusalem to see Peter, and abode with him fifteen days.

19 But other of the apostles saw I none, save James the Lord's brother.
20 Now the things which I write unto you, behold, before God, I lie not.
21 Afterwards I came into the regions of Syria and Cilicia;
22 And was unknown by face unto the churches of Judaea which were in Christ:
23 But they had heard only, That he which persecuted us in times past now preacheth the faith which once he destroyed.
24 And they glorified God in me.

Introduction

As we have learned, the book of Galatians was written to combat the false teachers who were attacking the apostle Paul and the validity of God's revelation through him. These false teachers were causing Galatian believers to turn back on their walk in Christ.

I. The Claim of Divine Revelation (vv. 11–12)

Paul was absolutely clear—the message he preached was from God.

A. Did Not Originate With Man (v. 11)

The word *certify* means "to declare a thing true, accurate, certain." The gospel preached by Paul was not a product of man. It was a certified truth given to him by the Holy Spirit.

The Rabinnical teachers or Judaizers diluted and added to Scripture. They emphasized man-made traditions over the truth of Scripture.

If the gospel Paul preached were from man, it would have been permeated with works.

B. Did Originate With God (v. 12)

In Acts 9, we read of Paul's encounter with Jesus on the road to Damascus. What we notice is that Jesus came directly to

Paul. Through special revelation to Paul on the Damascus road, God made known to man truth that was not previously known nor could be known without divine revelation.

1 Thessalonians 2:13

13 *For this cause also thank we God without ceasing, because, when ye received the word of God which ye heard of us, ye received it not as the word of men, but as it is in truth, the word of God, which effectually worketh also in you that believe.*

Note—When a person is saved, he begins to understand the Scripture. This is called *illumination*.

2 Corinthians 3:14–17

14 *But their minds were blinded: for until this day remaineth the same vail untaken away in the reading of the old testament; which vail is done away in Christ.*

15 *But even unto this day, when Moses is read, the vail is upon their heart.*

16 *Nevertheless when it shall turn to the Lord, the vail shall be taken away.*

17 *Now the Lord is that Spirit: and where the Spirit of the Lord is, there is liberty.*

II. The Comparison to Jewish Teachers

Paul uses his pre-conversion life to show his understanding of the Jewish doctrine and teachers.

A. *Paul's Persecution of the Churches (v. 13)*

Paul admits to two things:

- He was religious—"in the Jew's religion."
- He was intolerant of Christian beliefs—"how that beyond measure I persecuted the church of God, and wasted it."

Acts 8:3

8 As for Saul, he made havock of the church, entering into every house, and haling men and women committed them to prison.

Acts 26:11

11 And I punished them oft in every synagogue, and compelled them to blaspheme; and being exceedingly mad against them, I persecuted them even unto strange cities.

B. *Paul's Passion For Judaism (v. 14)*

As we read of Paul's experience with Judaism, we notice two things: he excelled (v.14a), and he was zealous (v. 14b). Before his salvation, Paul was not a casual student of his faith—he was a passionate fanatic about his Judaism.

Note—The word *traditions* in this passage denotes three ideas: oral teachings of the law, interpretations of the Torah, and ceremonial regulations.

Philippians 3:4–7

4 Though I might also have confidence in the flesh. If any other man thinketh that he hath whereof he might trust in the flesh, I more:

5 Circumcised the eighth day, of the stock of Israel, of the tribe of Benjamin, an Hebrew of the Hebrews; as touching the law, a Pharisee;

6 Concerning zeal, persecuting the church; touching the righteousness which is in the law, blameless.

7 But what things were gain to me, those I counted loss for Christ.

Because of his zeal for Judaism, grace was a foreign concept to Paul. The law commanded him to weed out heretical beliefs. Even the Jewish rulers of his day prodded him to follow through with this practice. But one encounter with God's amazing grace on the road to Damascus changed Paul forever.

Illustration—Grace is indeed the great changing factor of godless lives. John Newton, author of the hymn "Amazing Grace," is one of the best examples. Newton became the captain of a slave ship. But one night in a terrible storm, he trusted Christ as his Saviour. The grace of God transformed him into a godly pastor. His tombstone in Olney, England, reads: "John Newton, Clerk; once an infidel and libertine, a servant of slaves in Africa, was by the rich mercy of our Lord and Saviour Jesus Christ preserved, restored, pardoned, and appointed to preach the faith he had long labored to destroy."

III. The Calling to God's Purpose

How did this zealous follower of Judaism and persecutor of the church become the apostle to the Gentiles? It surely was a process, and Paul gives us an overview in verses 15–24.

A. *God's Man Was Sanctified (v. 15)*

JEREMIAH 1:5

5 Before I formed thee in the belly I knew thee; and before thou camest forth out of the womb I sanctified thee, and I ordained thee a prophet unto the nations.

According to grace (God's unmerited favor), Saul was converted, and according to God's plan Paul would reveal and preach Christ (v. 16). Just as God had a specific purpose for the Apostle Paul, God has a purpose for every Christian.

1 CORINTHIANS 15:10

10 But by the grace of God I am what I am: and his grace which was bestowed upon me was not in vain; but I laboured more abundantly than they all: yet not I, but the grace of God which was with me.

1 PETER 2:9

9 But ye are a chosen generation, a royal priesthood, an holy nation, a peculiar people; that ye should shew forth the

praises of him who hath called you out of darkness into his marvellous light:

B. God's Man Was Strengthened (vv. 16–24)
Here we see a chronology of Paul's preparation for ministry.

1. **Paul did not consult with flesh and blood (v. 16).**
2. **Paul spent time with Ananias in Damascus.**
3. **Paul went to Arabia and abode with God.**

   EPHESIANS 3:2–7
   2 *If ye have heard of the dispensation of the grace of God which is given me to youward:*
   3 *How that by revelation he made known unto me the mystery; (as I wrote afore in few words,*
   4 *Whereby, when ye read, ye may understand my knowledge in the mystery of Christ)*
   5 *Which in other ages was not made known unto the sons of men, as it is now revealed unto his holy apostles and prophets by the Spirit;*
   6 *That the Gentiles should be fellowheirs, and of the same body, and partakers of his promise in Christ by the gospel:*
   7 *Whereof I was made a minister, according to the gift of the grace of God given unto me by the effectual working of his power.*

4. **Paul returned to Damascus.**
   When Paul preached Christ, the Jews tried to kill him. After three years, he escaped from Damascus by being let down in a basket. He then went up to Jerusalem.

   ACTS 9:22–25
   22 *But Saul increased the more in strength, and confounded the Jews which dwelt at Damascus, proving that this is very Christ.*

> *23 And after that many days were fulfilled, the Jews took counsel to kill him:*
> *24 But their laying await was known of Saul. And they watched the gates day and night to kill him.*
> *25 Then the disciples took him by night, and let him down by the wall in a basket.*

5. **Paul went to Jerusalem and saw Peter.**

6. **After his encounter with Peter, Paul traveled to Syria and Cilicia (v. 21).**
   Tarsus was a city in Cilicia, and Antioch was in Syria. Tarsus (Saul's hometown) is where Barnabas found Saul then took him to Antioch.

   ACTS 11:25–26
   > *25 Then departed Barnabas to Tarsus, for to seek Saul:*
   > *26 And when he had found him, he brought him unto Antioch. And it came to pass, that a whole year they assembled themselves with the church, and taught much people. And the disciples were called Christians first in Antioch*

C. **God's Man Was Submitted (vv. 23–24)**
God specifically set Paul apart for the gospel ministry.

1. **To preaching (v. 23)**
   1 CORINTHIANS 1:18
   > *18 For the preaching of the cross is to them that perish foolishness; but unto us which are saved it is the power of God.*

2. **To God's glory (v. 24)**
   It was difficult for believers of this region to accept Paul's message. They were probably hesitant to trust him in the beginning, maybe even fearful to be in his presence, but

one thing motivated them to accept him: God would get the glory.

Conclusion

God's divine revelation will always end with God getting the glory for His own works. God often uses trying situations to bring about His glory in the end. In the life of the Apostle Paul, we see that through his conversion, separation, and even his persecution, God received the glory. Paul's life echoed the message of Christ that he preached. May our lives also support the message of our lips.

OUTLINE FOUR

IN DEFENSE OF GRACE
GALATIANS 2:1–10

1 Then fourteen years after I went up again to Jerusalem with Barnabas, and took Titus with me also.
2 And I went up by revelation, and communicated unto them that gospel which I preach among the Gentiles, but privately to them which were of reputation, lest by any means I should run, or had run, in vain.
3 But neither Titus, who was with me, being a Greek, was compelled to be circumcised:
4 And that because of false brethren unawares brought in, who came in privily to spy out our liberty which we have in Christ Jesus, that they might bring us into bondage:
5 To whom we gave place by subjection, no, not for an hour; that the truth of the gospel might continue with you.
6 But of these who seemed to be somewhat, (whatsoever they were, it maketh no matter to me: God accepteth no man's person:) for they who seemed to be somewhat in conference added nothing to me:
7 But contrariwise, when they saw that the gospel of the uncircumcision was committed unto me, as the gospel of the circumcision was unto Peter;

8 (For he that wrought effectually in Peter to the apostleship of the circumcision, the same was mighty in me toward the Gentiles:)
9 And when James, Cephas, and John, who seemed to be pillars, perceived the grace that was given unto me, they gave to me and Barnabas the right hands of fellowship; that we should go unto the heathen, and they unto the circumcision.
10 Only they would that we should remember the poor; the same which I also was forward to do.

Introduction

Throughout Paul's ministry he constantly fought against false teaching.

ACTS 20:28–30
28 Take heed therefore unto yourselves, and to all the flock, over the which the Holy Ghost hath made you overseers, to feed the church of God, which he hath purchased with his own blood.
29 For I know this, that after my departing shall grievous wolves enter in among you, not sparing the flock.
30 Also of your own selves shall men arise, speaking perverse things, to draw away disciples after them.

After he had planted the churches of Galatia, false teachers often called Judaizers were approaching new Christians with a mixture of grace and works for salvation. In this portion of Scripture, Paul shares with the Galatians news of his trip to Jerusalem to give background of his credibility.

I. Paul's Arrival at Jerusalem (vv. 1–2)

While all of the apostles were trained together under the ministry of Jesus, Paul had minimal contact with the other apostles. Paul's training happened in isolation in Arabia.

This trip to Jerusalem was possibly for the famous Jerusalem council of Acts 15. This may have happened after his first missionary journey which included traveling to Galatia.

A. His Destination

Paul's destination was to Jerusalem "to them which were of reputation" (v. 2). This would have included the Judaizers. The Judaizers had claimed Paul was of no reputation. Therefore, Paul is here vindicating his ministry.

Paul also privately shared what God had done with the leaders. The response of what he shared is shown in Acts 15.

ACTS 15:12
12 Then all the multitude kept silence, and gave audience to Barnabas and Paul, declaring what miracles and wonders God had wrought among the Gentiles by them.

B. His Delegation (v. 1)

1. Barnabas

Barnabas was Paul's dear friend who brought him from Tarsus to the church at Antioch.

Barnabas' attendance proves that this is the council of Jerusalem in Acts 15. Barnabas went with Paul because these two men were the missionary team. What Paul was to deal with concerning the Judaizers and the gospel, Barnabas would verify as well since he was on the missionary journey with Paul.

2. Titus

Titus was a Gentile convert, spiritual son of Paul, and one of his co-workers. Titus would testify of the fact of true conversion through grace alone, no works mixed in.

C. His Delivery (v. 2)

The phrase *by revelation* in Greek is *apokalypsis*, meaning "laying bear, making naked; a disclosure of truth, instruction concerning things before unknown."

Paul "went up by revelation," meaning not that God gave him a vision to go, but instead that he had received direct revelation from God concerning the gospel of grace (Galatians 1:11–12), and he was going to communicate this to the church at Jerusalem.

The gospel Paul preached among the Gentiles was of grace alone, and the authority by which he preached was based on the revelation Jesus Christ Himself gave to Paul. In essence, the revelation Paul received was the gospel itself.

ACTS 15:1–2
1   And certain men which came down from Judaea taught the brethren, and said, Except ye be circumcised after the manner of Moses, ye cannot be saved.
2   When therefore Paul and Barnabas had no small dissension and disputation with them, they determined that Paul and Barnabas, and certain other of them, should go up to Jerusalem unto the apostles and elders about this question.

II. Paul's Assistant in Ministry (vv. 3–5)

A. The Background of Titus

The name *Titus* (Titov, Titos) is of Latin origin. Titus might have been Greek by ethnicity, but the fact that his name is Latin not Greek indicates he may have been a Roman citizen. The term "Greek" was often used in a broader sense to include all Gentiles in comparison to the Jews. This would then imply that Titus may have been Roman and perhaps was from either Troas or Corinth. Titus was of great help to Paul later at the Corinthian church, and toward the end of Paul's life Titus was still faithfully serving Christ.

TITUS 1:4–5
4   To Titus, mine own son after the common faith: Grace, mercy, and peace, from God the Father and the Lord Jesus Christ our Saviour.

5 For this cause left I thee in Crete, that thou shouldest set in order the things that are wanting, and ordain elders in every city, as I had appointed thee:

2 Timothy 4:10

10 For Demas hath forsaken me, having loved this present world, and is departed unto Thessalonica; Crescens to Galatia, Titus unto Dalmatia.

B. *The Belief of Titus (v. 3)*

Paul makes special note when addressing the Galatian believers that when Titus (a Gentile convert to Christ) went to Jerusalem, he saw no need to submit to the Mosaic law and be circumcised. This would have sent a strong message that Christian believers did need to submit to the law.

Acts 15:10

10 Now therefore why tempt ye God, to put a yoke upon the neck of the disciples, which neither our fathers nor we were able to bear?

Acts 15:19

19 Wherefore my sentence is, that we trouble not them, which from among the Gentiles are turned to God:

Titus was a true Christian who did not need to prove a point by being circumcised. And if Paul had recommended the acts of the law such as circumcision, he would undercut his message of grace. Titus was living proof that the Judaizers taught a false gospel. Fulfilling the law did not bring peace; it only brought bondage to the law. However, trusting in Christ's grace brought to Titus peace and assurance that the Judaizers could not promise.

III. Paul's Answer to the Judaizers

A. *Their Profession Was False (v. 4)*
The Judaizers claimed the grace of Christ, but they tainted it with the works of the law.

GALATIANS 5:2–4
2   Behold, I Paul say unto you, that if ye be circumcised, Christ shall profit you nothing.
3   For I testify again to every man that is circumcised, that he is a debtor to do the whole law.
4   Christ is become of no effect unto you, whosoever of you are justified by the law; ye are fallen from grace.

Some believe these pseudo-Christians were actually planted in the churches by the Pharisees to cause disruption among the members.

B. *Their Perception Was False (v. 4)*
The Judaizer's perception on grace and the law brought bondage, not liberty. However, Paul's message from Christ brought liberty in two ways: from the law and from sin's penalty.

ROMANS 8:2
2   For the law of the Spirit of life in Christ Jesus hath made me free from the law of sin and death.

C. *Their Presence Should be Forsaken (v. 5)*
Paul claims that he and those around him did not subject themselves to these Judaizers' teachings, "no, not for an hour." Paul worked with weak Christians, but he refused to make any concession for false teachers. This decision would have been difficult because these false teachers purported to be brothers.

2 Thessalonians 3:6

6 *Now we command you, brethren, in the name of our Lord Jesus Christ, that ye withdraw yourselves from every brother that walketh disorderly, and not after the tradition which he received of us.*

IV. Paul's Acceptance of Responsibility (vv. 6–10)

A. *Was Seen By Those in Reputation (vv. 6–7)*

Paul exclaims that his teaching being seen by those in reputation "added nothing to him." In other words, he did not need their approval.

2 Corinthians 12:11

11 *I am become a fool in glorying; ye have compelled me: for I ought to have been commended of you: for in nothing am I behind the very chiefest apostles, though I be nothing.*

Paul's reassurance of his life and his work came only from Christ.

B. *Was Serious To Paul (v. 6c)*

The twelve apostles had not confirmed the importance of the gospel to Paul. He knew it.

Note—Whether others see the gospel or your calling as important is not as important as you knowing it!

C. *Was Supported By the Brethren (vv. 9–10)*

Peter, James, and John showed their acceptance of Paul and Barnabas as partners in ministry by giving them their "right hands of fellowship."

Colossians 1:29

29 *Whereunto I also labour, striving according to his working, which worketh in me mightily.*

Acts 15:22–24

22 *Then pleased it the apostles and elders, with the whole church, to send chosen men of their own company to Antioch with Paul and Barnabas; namely, Judas surnamed Barsabas, and Silas, chief men among the brethren:*

23 *And they wrote letters by them after this manner; The apostles and elders and brethren send greeting unto the brethren which are of the Gentiles in Antioch and Syria and Cilicia:*

24 *Forasmuch as we have heard, that certain which went out from us have troubled you with words, subverting your souls, saying, Ye must be circumcised, and keep the law: to whom we gave no such commandment:*

The only advice Peter, James, and John had for Paul was to remember the poor (v. 10).

Conclusion

Paul did all he did for the Lord and for the simplicity of the gospel. Although he was criticized by the Jewish rulers, he endured. Although others sought the acceptance of those with reputation, he stayed his course. Even when he received little encouragement from other believers, Paul remained faithful to the message of Christ's gospel.

OUTLINE FIVE

JUSTIFIED BY FAITH
GALATIANS 2:11–19

11 But when Peter was come to Antioch, I withstood him to the face, because he was to be blamed.
12 For before that certain came from James, he did eat with the Gentiles: but when they were come, he withdrew and separated himself, fearing them which were of the circumcision.
13 And the other Jews dissembled likewise with him; insomuch that Barnabas also was carried away with their dissimulation.
14 But when I saw that they walked not uprightly according to the truth of the gospel, I said unto Peter before them all, If thou, being a Jew, livest after the manner of Gentiles, and not as do the Jews, why compellest thou the Gentiles to live as do the Jews?
15 We who are Jews by nature, and not sinners of the Gentiles,
16 Knowing that a man is not justified by the works of the law, but by the faith of Jesus Christ, even we have believed in Jesus Christ, that we might be justified by the faith of Christ, and not by the works of the law: for by the works of the law shall no flesh be justified.

17 But if, while we seek to be justified by Christ, we ourselves also are found sinners, is therefore Christ the minister of sin? God forbid.
18 For if I build again the things which I destroyed, I make myself a transgressor.
19 For I through the law am dead to the law, that I might live unto God.

Introduction

As we come to this portion of chapter 2, Paul continues to explain the difficulties of living by the law in order to be saved or to maintain salvation. These teachings, being promoted by the Judaizers, were even causing good men to falter or hesitate in their Christian walk.

GALATIANS 1:6–7
6 I marvel that ye are so soon removed from him that called you into the grace of Christ unto another gospel:
7 Which is not another; but there be some that trouble you, and would pervert the gospel of Christ.

Satan is always trying to push us back. He may use unbelievers, backslidden believers, or even well-intentioned believers we trust to try to make us falter in our Christian walk.

I. Paul's Contention with Peter (vv. 11–12)

In these verses Paul continues to defend his apostleship and authority that the Judaizers were trying to discredit.

A. *Paul's Position for Truth (v. 11)*

Verse 11 says that Paul "withstood Peter." The word *withstood* means "to set one's self against, to withstand, resist, oppose; to set against."

Notice the way Paul "withstood Peter." He withstood him "to the face." There was no malicious backbiting or slander here. Paul directly told Peter his fault.

Illustration—My name is Gossip. I have no respect for justice. I maim without killing. I break hearts and ruin lives. I am cunning and malicious and gather strength with age. The more I am quoted, the more I am believed.

My victims are helpless. They cannot protect themselves against me because I have no name and face. To track me down is impossible. The harder you try, the more elusive I become. I am nobody's friend.

Once I tarnish a reputation, it is never the same. I topple governments and wreck marriages. I make headlines and headaches. I ruin careers and cause sleepless nights, heartaches and indigestion. I make innocent people cry in their pillows. Even my name hisses. I am called Gossip.—Author Unknown

Quote—Leonard Ravenhill once wrote, "We never pray for folks we gossip about, and we never gossip about the folks for whom we pray!"

The phrase *he was to be blamed* is *kataginosko* in Greek, meaning, "to find fault with, blame." Peter was guilty of blame in this circumstance; therefore, Paul confronted him face to face to deal with the problem. This is the biblical example of the way we are to deal with grievances.

Matthew 18:15
15 *Moreover if thy brother shall trespass against thee, go and tell him his fault between thee and him alone: if he shall hear thee, thou hast gained thy brother.*

B. *Peter's Place with the Gentiles (v. 12b)*
Peter was fellowshipping with the Gentile believers at the church in Antioch, but when other Jews sent by James from Jerusalem showed up, Peter suddenly separated himself from the Gentile believers. This act in effect supported the Judaizers' position in belittling Paul's teaching of salvation by grace alone through faith alone.

By Peter's withdrawing from the Gentiles, he caused other Jews who were watching to follow suit. Peter's decision was motivated solely by fear.

GALATIANS 2:12
> 12 ...*But when they were come, he withdrew and separated himself, fearing them which were of the circumcision.*

C. Paul's Problem with Compromise (vv. 13–14)
Paul's problem with compromise was that it affected others. Even Barnabas was influenced by Peter!

II. Paul's Case for the Gospel (vv. 15–16)
Paul did not only rebuke Peter for discrediting the grace of the gospel; he explained what the gospel is and why the keeping of the law undermines it.

A. The Way of Justification

1. **Not by works (v. 16a)**

   Illustration—Sometimes we fool ourselves into thinking we have control of our circumstances. A little girl was asked in Sunday School, "Who made you?" And she said, "Well, God made part of me." "What do you mean God made part of you?" "Well, God made me real little, and I just growed the rest myself."

   ROMANS 3:20
   > 20 *Therefore by the deeds of the law there shall no flesh be justified in his sight: for by the law is the knowledge of sin.*

   TITUS 3:5
   > 5 *Not by works of righteousness which we have done, but according to his mercy he saved us, by the washing of regeneration, and renewing of the Holy Ghost;*

2. **By Faith (v. 16b)**
   ROMANS 3:21–22
   21 *But now the righteousness of God without the law is manifested, being witnessed by the law and the prophets;*
   22 *Even the righteousness of God which is by faith of Jesus Christ unto all and upon all them that believe: for there is no difference:*

B. ***The Work of Justification (v. 16)***
   Christ did the work of justification for us.

   1 JOHN 2:1–2
   1 *My little children, these things write I unto you, that ye sin not. And if any man sin, we have an advocate with the Father, Jesus Christ the righteous:*
   2 *And he is the propitiation for our sins: and not for ours only, but also for the sins of the whole world.*

   Illustration—The old hymn, "Through the Love of God Our Saviour" says, "Precious is the blood that healed us; perfect is the grace that sealed us; strong the hand stretched forth to shield us. All must be well."

III. Paul's Commentary on the Situation (vv. 17–19)

A. ***Christ Does Not Cause Sin (v. 17)***
   1 JOHN 3:5
   5 *And ye know that he was manifested to take away our sins; and in him is no sin.*

   Note—We do not want to frustrate the grace of God!

   Clarke's commentary on this verse explains it this way: "If, while we acknowledge that we must be justified by faith in Christ, we ourselves are found sinners, enjoining the necessity of observing the rites and ceremonies of the law, we thus constitute ourselves sinners; is, therefore, Christ the minister of sin? Christ, who has taught us to renounce the law, and expect justification through his death? God forbid! that we should either act so, or think so."

B. We Must Not Cause Doubt (vv. 18–19)
1 CORINTHIANS 14:8

8 For if the trumpet give an uncertain sound, who shall prepare himself to the battle?

Paul explains that he cannot force the Gentiles to observe the law because he has claimed Christ's death to be satisfactory separate from the law. If he promotes the observance of the law, he will build back up the very teachings he has destroyed.

He continues to explain in verse 19 that believers do not need to depend on the law.

Conclusion

In our day, the issue is not Judaism. But even today, every false religion in some way diminishes the grace of God by adding works for salvation. We must hold to the truth that we are justified by faith alone!

OUTLINE SIX

CHRIST LIVETH IN ME
GALATIANS 2:20–21

20 *I am crucified with Christ: nevertheless I live; yet not I, but Christ liveth in me: and the life which I now live in the flesh I live by the faith of the Son of God, who loved me, and gave himself for me.*

21 *I do not frustrate the grace of God: for if righteousness come by the law, then Christ is dead in vain.*

In previous verses, Paul showed Peter the folly of going back to the law. Paul's contention with Peter was over salvation by faith in Christ. By reverting back to the law, Peter was implying that he was still needing to be saved and that Christ did not save him. Paul clearly stated that Christians no longer need to trust in the law because we trust in the sacrifice of Christ.

Verses 20–21 confirm this and draw this truth to its interaction with our daily lives. Not only can we not save ourselves, but we cannot manufacture the spiritual life. It is the life of Christ in us that allows us to live according to the gospel of grace.

I. The Believer's Position

The Christian life is designed to be a life of unity and union with Christ. Because we are "in Christ," we share His death and resurrection. In Christ, the enthronement of self ends.

A. Identification with Christ

By using the phrase, "I am crucified with Christ," Paul identified himself with Christ's death on the cross. Paul had tried to find life through the keeping and works of the law but instead found death by the law. Paul found that life came to him through Christ's death for the payment for sin, something the law could never do.

In Christ we have died to the demands and jurisdictions of the law. By the death of Christ upon the cross we have become utterly estranged from (dead to) our former habits of feeling and action. We now have the ability to reckon ourselves dead to sin, self, and our carnal tendencies and live in the power of the resurrection.

ROMANS 6:11
11 *Likewise reckon ye also yourselves to be dead indeed unto sin, but alive unto God through Jesus Christ our Lord.*

B. Identification with the Cross

By identifying with Christ's death, Paul was changed.

ROMANS 6:3–6
3 *Know ye not, that so many of us as were baptized into Jesus Christ were baptized into his death?*
4 *Therefore we are buried with him by baptism into death: that like as Christ was raised up from the dead by the glory of the Father, even so we also should walk in newness of life.*
5 *For if we have been planted together in the likeness of his death, we shall be also in the likeness of his resurrection:*

> 6 Knowing this, that our old man is crucified with him, that the body of sin might be destroyed, that henceforth we should not serve sin.

Paul does not emphasize trying to obey the law but rather reckoning who he is in Christ. Paul says that he is a crucified dead man.

- A dead man does not try to obey the law—he's dead.
- A dead man does not try to battle the world—he's dead.
- A dead man is not controlled by sin—he's dead.

GALATIANS 5:24
> 24 And they that are Christ's have crucified the flesh with the affections and lusts.

GALATIANS 6:14–15
> 14 But God forbid that I should glory, save in the cross of our Lord Jesus Christ, by whom the world is crucified unto me, and I unto the world.

II. The Believer's Passion

As Paul recognized the truth that his old man was crucified with Christ, he expressed his passion to live for God—"nevertheless I live!"

God does not expect the Christian life to be lived by the ability and power of the flesh, but by the power of the living Spirit of God. The indwelling Spirit gives us a passion to live for God moment by moment.

A. *Passionate about the Resurrection*

As we consider our identity in Christ, realize that when Christ took His stand on eternal ground, we were standing there with Him!

Paul proclaimed "nevertheless I live." Paul was alive, yet he was not alive in himself but in Christ. Paul realized that he was now a man alive unto God and would be controlled, influenced, and directed by Him.

B. Passionate about Living in Christ

Because we are dead in and of ourselves and because Christ gave us life, we should passionately live for Him.

COLOSSIANS 3:3–4
3   For ye are dead, and your life is hid with Christ in God.
4   When Christ, who is our life, shall appear, then shall ye also appear with him in glory.

III. The Believer's Power

The Holy Spirit gives us a passionate hunger to experience the daily presence of God. Galatians 2:20 reminds us that we don't live the Christian life in our own strength, but "Christ liveth in me." This identifies us with Christ's power.

Illustration—In the book *Lectures to My Students*, Charles Spurgeon wrote, "When your own emptiness is painfully forced upon your consciousness, chide yourself that you ever dreamed of being full except in the Lord."

A. Not through Self

JOHN 15:5
5   I am the vine, ye are the branches: He that abideth in me, and I in him, the same bringeth forth much fruit: for without me ye can do nothing.

B. But through Christ

The true Christian life is not so much a believer's living for Christ as Christ's living through the believer.

Quote— Jesus died on the cross to save you from sin. He lives in you to save you from self.

COLOSSIANS 1:27
27 To whom God would make known what is the riches of the glory of this mystery among the Gentiles; which is Christ in you, the hope of glory:

2 PETER 1:4
4 Whereby are given unto us exceeding great and precious promises: that by these ye might be partakers of the divine nature, having escaped the corruption that is in the world through lust.

EPHESIANS 3:17
17 That Christ may dwell in your hearts by faith; that ye, being rooted and grounded in love,

PHILIPPIANS 4:13
13 I can do all things through Christ which strengtheneth me.

Illustration—Theologians tell a story to illustrate how Christ's triumph benefits our lives. Imagine a city under siege. The enemy that surrounds the city will not let anyone or anything leave. Supplies are running low, and the citizens are fearful. But in the dark of the night, a spy sneaks through the enemy lines. He has rushed to the city to tell the people that in another place the main enemy force has been defeated; the leaders have already surrendered. The people do not need to be afraid. It is only a matter of time until the besieging troops receive the news and lay down their weapons. Similarly, we may seem now to be surrounded by the forces of evil—disease, injustice, oppression, death. But the enemy has actually been defeated at Calvary. Things are not the way they seem to be. It is only a matter of time until it becomes clear to all that the battle is really over.

IV. The Believer's Persuasion (v. 20c)

Paul explained in the last part of verse 20 why he lives.

A. *I Live by Faith*

How do we daily live out the life of Christ? By faith. Christ's incredible sacrifice for us motivates us to live for Him by faith.

2 Corinthians 5:7

7   *(For we walk by faith, not by sight:)*

The Lord often allows us to endure affliction or adversity that He might develop our faith. We don't enjoy these times, and we would never choose them on our own. Yet, the Lord uses them to strengthen and develop our faith and to deepen our hunger for His presence.

Quote—Hudson Taylor once said, "Many Christians estimate difficulties in the light of their own resources, and thus attempt little and often fail in the little they attempt. All God's giants have been weak men who did great things for God because they reckoned on His power and presence with them."

Romans 5:2

2   *By whom also we have access by faith into this grace wherein we stand, and rejoice in hope of the glory of God.*

Believers should live by the element of faith, not the element of flesh.

B. *I Live because of His Love*

Paul said he lived by the faith of the Son of God "who loved me, and gave himself for me." When we consider His love for us, how can we not live by faith?

Ephesians 5:25

25 *Husbands, love your wives, even as Christ also loved the church, and gave himself for it;*

Romans 8:37–39

37 *Nay, in all these things we are more than conquerors through him that loved us.*

38 *For I am persuaded, that neither death, nor life, nor angels, nor principalities, nor powers, nor things present, nor things to come,*

39 *Nor height, nor depth, nor any other creature, shall be able to separate us from the love of God, which is in Christ Jesus our Lord.*

Conclusion

Our lives in Christ always begin with our position; our position then feeds our passion, power, and persuasion.

Verse 21 concludes this chapter by emphasizing that we are sustained by grace alone. It would be needless for Christ to go to the cross and die if the law could obtain righteousness for the sinner. Obviously, the law was not able to produce in man righteousness that would be acceptable to God. The law can only condemn the sinner. However, it is the grace of God that saves and sustains a sinner through the sacrifice of Jesus Christ.

Outline Seven

Continuing in the Spirit
Galatians 3:1–5

1 O foolish Galatians, who hath bewitched you, that ye should not obey the truth, before whose eyes Jesus Christ hath been evidently set forth, crucified among you?
2 This only would I learn of you, Received ye the Spirit by the works of the law, or by the hearing of faith?
3 Are ye so foolish? having begun in the Spirit, are ye now made perfect by the flesh?
4 Have ye suffered so many things in vain? if it be yet in vain.
5 He therefore that ministereth to you the Spirit, and worketh miracles among you, doeth he it by the works of the law, or by the hearing of faith?

Introduction

Few things are more tragic or disappointing than a Christian who deserts the purity of the gospel for a false form of Christianity that presumes to improve on the finished work of Christ. Yet that is what many believers in the Galatian churches had done or were in danger of doing because of the Judaizers.

Galatians 1:6–7

6 *I marvel that ye are so soon removed from him that called you into the grace of Christ unto another gospel:*
7 *Which is not another; but there be some that trouble you, and would pervert the gospel of Christ.*

I. The Problem of the Galatians (v. 1)

A. *They Were Foolish*

Paul was incredulous, hardly able to believe what the Galatians had done. The Galatians had been lazy and undiscerning. They had foolishly fallen into Judaistic legalism because they had stopped believing and applying the basic truths of the gospel Paul had taught them and by which they had been saved. By sinful neglect of their divine resources, they compromised the gospel of grace.

Ephesians 5:15–16

15 *See then that ye walk circumspectly, not as fools, but as wise,*
16 *Redeeming the time, because the days are evil.*

Note—The obedient Christian experiences joy and satisfaction beyond measure, far exceeding that of superficial believers who constantly seek spiritual "highs."

B. *They Were Fooled*

The word *bewitched* means that the Galatians were charmed. Essentially, they had trusted feeling over fact.

What happened with the Galatians is still Satan's goal today. He wants to seduce believers to follow false doctrine.

2 Corinthians 11:3–4

3 *But I fear, lest by any means, as the serpent beguiled Eve through his subtilty, so your minds should be corrupted from the simplicity that is in Christ.*

4 For if he that cometh preacheth another Jesus, whom we have not preached, or if ye receive another spirit, which ye have not received, or another gospel, which ye have not accepted, ye might well bear with him.

GALATIANS 5:7
7 Ye did run well; who did hinder you that ye should not obey the truth?

C. They Were Fickle

The Galatians had clearly seen the truth set forth before their very eyes (v. 1c). However, they were fickle in their beliefs, changing from what they knew to be true back to a ritual religiosity. The truth they turned from was that they needed nothing other than Jesus Christ to gain salvation.

1 CORINTHIANS 2:2
2 For I determined not to know any thing among you, save Jesus Christ, and him crucified.

Even today, the power of the cross is enough. No ritual, ceremony, regulation, or any other thing devised or accomplished by men can pick up where the cross leaves off—because the cross never leaves off. The cross is the continuing and eternal payment for all sin, and every sinner who puts his trust in the cross is forever and continually forgiven. However, the person who puts his trust in the law obligates himself to keep the entire law, which is humanly impossible.

II. The Priority of Faith (vv. 2–4)

A. By Faith We Are Saved (v. 2)

The Galatians received the righteousness of Christ and His Holy Spirit at the time of their salvation. They must have known the Holy Spirit's unmistakable presence. So why would they revert to the law, something that left man with a lack of peace and hope?

Romans 8:16

16 *The Spirit itself beareth witness with our spirit, that we are the children of God:*

1 John 4:13

13 *Hereby know we that we dwell in him, and he in us, because he hath given us of his Spirit.*

Note—Just as we do not receive the Spirit by works, we do not remain saved through works.

B. By Faith We Continue in the Spirit (vv. 3–4)

We are given the Holy Spirit at salvation, and then we are to mature spiritually through the work of the Holy Spirit.

The validity of good works in God's sight depends on whose power they are done in and whose glory they are done for. We are saved by the Spirit, and the Bible commands us to walk in the Spirit. If we walk in the Spirit, our good works will be solely for God's honor and not our own validation.

Galatians 5:16–17

16 *This I say then, Walk in the Spirit, and ye shall not fulfill the lust of the flesh.*

17 *For the flesh lusteth against the Spirit, and the Spirit against the flesh: and these are contrary the one to the other: so that ye cannot do the things that ye would.*

III. The Power of the Lord (v. 5)

Continuing growth and spiritual service in our Christian life is not possible through our power; it is only by the power of the Lord that we continue in Him.

A. The Reception of the Spirit Is by Christ.

JOHN 16:13

13 *Howbeit when he, the Spirit of truth, is come, he will guide you into all truth: for he shall not speak of himself; but whatsoever he shall hear, that shall he speak: and he will shew you things to come.*

B. The Revelation of the Miraculous Is by Christ.

Fruit such as souls, repentance, and offerings are not our fruit to claim. They are the fruit of the Spirit. We as believers are only commanded to abide in Christ, and in Him we will bear much fruit.

JOHN 15:5

5 *I am the vine, ye are the branches: He that abideth in me, and I in him, the same bringeth forth much fruit: for without me ye can do nothing.*

1 CORINTHIANS 2:4

4 *And my speech and my preaching was not with enticing words of man's wisdom, but in demonstration of the Spirit and of power:*

Paul's message was that only through Christ could powerful and wonderful things be done.

Conclusion

Through the law, man had no hope. Through Christ, man had eternal hope, the promise of salvation, and the power of the Holy Spirit. The Galatians foolishly and lazily abandoned the truth of the gospel for a message of condemnation and hopelessness. Paul reminded them that their hope through Jesus Christ was still alive and ready to be reclaimed.

OUTLINE EIGHT

THE FAMILY OF FAITH
GALATIANS 3:6–14

6 Even as Abraham believed God, and it was accounted to him for righteousness.

7 Know ye therefore that they which are of faith, the same are the children of Abraham.

8 And the scripture, foreseeing that God would justify the heathen through faith, preached before the gospel unto Abraham, saying, In thee shall all nations be blessed.

9 So then they which be of faith are blessed with faithful Abraham.

10 For as many as are of the works of the law are under the curse: for it is written, Cursed is every one that continueth not in all things which are written in the book of the law to do them.

11 But that no man is justified by the law in the sight of God, it is evident: for, The just shall live by faith.

12 And the law is not of faith: but, The man that doeth them shall live in them.

13 Christ hath redeemed us from the curse of the law, being made a curse for us: for it is written, Cursed is every one that hangeth on a tree:

14 *That the blessing of Abraham might come on the Gentiles through Jesus Christ; that we might receive the promise of the Spirit through faith.*

Introduction

At the crux of the issue in the lives of Galatian believers was the question of salvation through works or through grace through faith in Christ. To show the Galatians the importance of faith, Paul takes them back to Abraham and his faith in following God.

I. The Faith of Abraham

A. *Abraham Believed (v. 6)*
GENESIS 12:1–3

1 Now the LORD had said unto Abram, Get thee out of thy country, and from thy kindred, and from thy father's house, unto a land that I will shew thee:

2 And I will make of thee a great nation, and I will bless thee, and make thy name great; and thou shalt be a blessing:

3 And I will bless them that bless thee, and curse him that curseth thee: and in thee shall all families of the earth be blessed.

B. *Abraham Received Imputed Righteousness (v. 6)*
GENESIS 15:6

6 And he believed in the LORD; and he counted it to him for righteousness.

The Old Testament saints, such as Abraham, were saved by faith, the same as New Testament saints. The Old Testament saints' faith was based on the revelation of truth that God had given them concerning salvation up to that point.

The word *accounted* means "placed on our account, reckoned." The accounting of righteousness to Abraham was through faith. This took place about fourteen years before God gave

Abraham the sign of circumcision. This is important because the Judaizers were insisting that believers must be circumcised to complete their salvation.

ROMANS 4:1–3
1 What shall we say then that Abraham our father, as pertaining to the flesh, hath found?
2 For if Abraham were justified by works, he hath whereof to glory; but not before God.
3 For what saith the scripture? Abraham believed God, and it was counted unto him for righteousness.

ROMANS 4:9–11
9 Cometh this blessedness then upon the circumcision only, or upon the uncircumcision also? for we say that faith was reckoned to Abraham for righteousness.
10 How was it then reckoned? when he was in circumcision, or in uncircumcision? Not in circumcision, but in uncircumcision.
11 And he received the sign of circumcision, a seal of the righteousness of the faith which he had yet being uncircumcised: that he might be the father of all them that believe, though they be not circumcised; that righteousness might be imputed unto them also:

In Romans 4:11, the word *seal* is *sphragis* in Greek, meaning, "that by which anything is confirmed, proved, authenticated, as by a seal (a token or proof)." Circumcision was only the token, proof, or mark—not the means of salvation.

Today, the seal of salvation is the Holy Spirit.

EPHESIANS 1:12–13
12 That we should be to the praise of his glory, who first trusted in Christ.
13 In whom ye also trusted, after that ye heard the word of truth, the gospel of your salvation: in whom also after that ye believed, ye were sealed with that holy Spirit of promise,

II. The Family of Abraham

Those of us who put our faith in Christ are of the same family of faith as Abraham. The family of Abraham has two similar qualities:

A. They Believe (v. 7)

EPHESIANS 2:8–9

8 For by grace are ye saved through faith; and that not of yourselves: it is the gift of God:

9 Not of works, lest any man should boast.

B. They Receive Justification (vv. 8–9)

1. **The recipients qualified (v. 8)**

    Paul now claims anyone who is of faith is part of the family of Abraham. This would be the family of all the saved. Even we today are the spiritual children of Abraham described in verse 8.

    When God gave Abraham His covenant in Genesis 12:1–3, one of the promises of that covenant was "and in thee shall all families of the earth be blessed" (v. 3).

    GENESIS 18:18

    18 Seeing that Abraham shall surely become a great and mighty nation, and all the nations of the earth shall be blessed in him?

    GALATIANS 3:28–29

    28 There is neither Jew nor Greek, there is neither bond nor free, there is neither male nor female: for ye are all one in Christ Jesus.

    29 And if ye be Christ's, then are ye Abraham's seed, and heirs according to the promise.

2. **The request fulfilled (v. 9)**

Therefore all who have put faith in Jesus Christ as their Saviour are also blessed by Abraham's "seed," Jesus Christ, who is the Saviour of all men, especially of those who believe.

1 Timothy 4:10
10 *For therefore we both labour and suffer reproach, because we trust in the living God, who is the Saviour of all men, specially of those that believe.*

Ephesians 1:7
7 *In whom we have redemption through his blood, the forgiveness of sins, according to the riches of his grace;*

III. The Favor of God (vv. 10–14)

All man-made religions teach that the favor of God is obtained through some sort of works. Yet Scripture plainly teaches otherwise.

A.   *Is Not Found in the Law (vv. 10–12)*

The Judaizers strongly advocated the necessity of keeping the Mosaic law in order to be saved. Once again, God made it clear in the Old Testament that this demand could never be kept for three reasons:

1. **The law required perfection (v. 10).**
   There is no doubt that God's law is perfect: it is without flaw. However, if a person is to come to God by the law, he also must be perfect in the keeping of it: he also must be flawless.

   Deuteronomy 27:26
   26 *Cursed be he that confirmeth not all the words of this law to do them. And all the people shall say, Amen.*

Ezekiel 18:4

4 Behold, all souls are mine; as the soul of the father, so also the soul of the son is mine: the soul that sinneth, it shall die.

James 2:10–11

10 For whosoever shall keep the whole law, and yet offend in one point, he is guilty of all.

11 For he that said, Do not commit adultery, said also, Do not kill. Now if thou commit no adultery, yet if thou kill, thou art become a transgressor of the law.

2. **The law did not justify (v. 11).**

The law cannot produce any fruit unto life. Paul says in verse 11 that no man can be justified by the law. This is obvious because no man can meet up to the law's qualifications. In fact, meeting the law's qualifications was never God's intent for us. He knew justification could only come by grace through faith because "the just shall live by faith" (v. 11).

The law only confirmed and gave knowledge to man of his sinfulness and guilt.

Romans 3:20

20 Therefore by the deeds of the law there shall no flesh be justified in his sight: for by the law is the knowledge of sin.

God knew the law could not produce the fruit of salvation. Salvation could only come by grace through faith. The law only pointed to righteousness, but Christ justified us with His own righteousness.

3. **The law is not of faith (v. 12–14).**

Attempting to keep the law requires no faith (v. 12). Yet our salvation must be through faith in Christ, for it is He who has redeemed us from the curse of the law (v. 13).

When we trust Christ by faith, He redeems us, and the Spirit secures us (v. 14).

Ephesians 1:7
7 In whom we have redemption through his blood, the forgiveness of sins, according to the riches of his grace;

Ephesians 1:13–14
13 In whom ye also trusted, after that ye heard the word of truth, the gospel of your salvation: in whom also after that ye believed, ye were sealed with that holy Spirit of promise,
14 Which is the earnest of our inheritance until the redemption of the purchased possession, unto the praise of his glory.

B. *Is Found in Christ (vv. 13–14)*
While the favor of God is not found in the law, it is found in Christ!

1. **Christ has redeemed us (v. 13).**
   We could never earn God's favor or our salvation on our own. Jesus has redeemed us with His blood.

   Ephesians 1:7
   7 In whom we have redemption through his blood, the forgiveness of sins, according to the riches of his grace;

2. **The Spirit has secured us (v. 14).**
   The "promise of the Spirit" is that we are sealed forever.

   Ephesians 1:13–14
   13 In whom ye also trusted, after that ye heard the word of truth, the gospel of your salvation: in whom also after that ye believed, ye were sealed with that holy Spirit of promise,

> 14 Which is the earnest of our inheritance until the redemption of the purchased possession, unto the praise of his glory.

Conclusion

As part of Abraham's family of faith, we have a message. It's the same message that was given to Abraham, the same message that Paul preached, and the same message that we were saved by: the message of salvation by grace through faith alone. Christ's perfect work on the cross justifies us in the sight of God if we only believe. Our feeble works or attempts to keep the law always fall short of God's glory. We only need to trust in the blood of our High Priest, Jesus Christ, to be saved. It is this message of faith that we must share with those still seeking their works for justification.

HEBREWS 9:11–12

> 11 But Christ being come an high priest of good things to come, by a greater and more perfect tabernacle, not made with hands, that is to say, not of this building;
> 12 Neither by the blood of goats and calves, but by his own blood he entered in once into the holy place, having obtained eternal redemption for us.

OUTLINE NINE

THE PROMISE OF FAITH
GALATIANS 3:15–25

15 Brethren, I speak after the manner of men; Though it be but a man's covenant, yet if it be confirmed, no man disannulleth, or addeth thereto.
16 Now to Abraham and his seed were the promises made. He saith not, And to seeds, as of many; but as of one, And to thy seed, which is Christ.
17 And this I say, that the covenant, that was confirmed before of God in Christ, the law, which was four hundred and thirty years after, cannot disannul, that it should make the promise of none effect.
18 For if the inheritance be of the law, it is no more of promise: but God gave it to Abraham by promise.
19 Wherefore then serveth the law? It was added because of transgressions, till the seed should come to whom the promise was made; and it was ordained by angels in the hand of a mediator.
20 Now a mediator is not a mediator of one, but God is one.
21 Is the law then against the promises of God? God forbid: for if there had been a law given which could have given life, verily righteousness should have been by the law.
22 But the scripture hath concluded all under sin, that the promise by faith of Jesus Christ might be given to them that believe.

23 But before faith came, we were kept under the law, shut up unto the faith which should afterwards be revealed.

24 Wherefore the law was our schoolmaster to bring us unto Christ, that we might be justified by faith.

25 But after that faith is come, we are no longer under a schoolmaster.

Introduction

In Galatians 3:1–14, we saw that Paul proved from the Old Testament that Abraham was justified by faith and not by the law. Every other believer then, whether Jew or Gentile, is also saved by faith alone. This principle was made effective by the shed blood of Jesus Christ, which paid for the sin curse that is upon every person.

In this next passage, Paul anticipates the Judaizers next objection. Paul understood that Abraham and all his descendants, prior to Sinai, were saved by faith, but then God gave Moses the law at Mount Sinai. So after the law was given it was necessary to include it as either a replacement of faith or a supplement with faith.

Therefore the Judaizer's conclusion is that Abraham and those earlier were saved by faith alone because there was no law. But then came the law which changed things. Why else would God have given the law if it is not for salvation? What is the purpose of the law?

Paul gives three arguments to answer these questions:

I. The Reliability of the Covenant (vv. 15–18)

Here Paul references the promise God made to Abraham. Specifically, he shows how reliable it was and how it was fulfilled by Christ.

A. *Man's Promise Illustrated (v. 15)*

1. **The illustration**—*"Brethren, I speak after the manner of men; Though it be but a man's covenant…"*

The word *covenant* means "an arrangement." This word is used to refer in general to a binding contract like a last will and testament. The illustration is that when a contract or agreement is made by people involving obligations and promises, no one can add to it or take from it. It will remain as it was originally made.

2. **The importance**—*"...yet if it be confirmed, no man disannulleth, or addeth thereto."*

    If man honors covenants made between men or made by a man, then how much more will God honor His Word when He makes a covenant? The testimony of God is that He cannot lie and that He is immutable; therefore what He promises will not falter or be changed.

B. *God's Promise Imputed (v. 16)*

1. **The Abrahamic Covenant was unconditional.**
    When God gave Abraham His promises, He swore by His own name.

    HEBREWS 6:17–19
    17 Wherein God, willing more abundantly to shew unto the heirs of promise the immutability of his counsel, confirmed it by an oath:
    18 That by two immutable things, in which it was impossible for God to lie, we might have a strong consolation, who have fled for refuge to lay hold upon the hope set before us:
    19 Which hope we have as an anchor of the soul, both sure and stedfast, and which entereth into that within the veil;

2. **The Abrahamic Covenant was specific.**
    When God gave Abraham His promises, they were specific. So it was when God gave the first promise of a Messiah to Adam and Eve.

Genesis 3:15

15 And I will put enmity between thee and the woman, and between thy seed and her seed; it shall bruise thy head, and thou shalt bruise his heel.

Whether before or after Christ came to earth, salvation has always been provided only through the perfect offering of Christ on the cross. Believers who lived before the cross and never knew specifics about Jesus were nevertheless forgiven and made right with God by faith in anticipation of Christ's sacrifice; whereas believers who live after the cross are saved in looking back to it.

C. *God's Promise Confirmed (by Christ) (vv. 17–18)*

The law, which came 430 years after the Abrahamic covenant, does not invalidate a covenant previously ratified by God. Because the covenant with Abraham was permanent and inviolate, no amount of time could nullify the promise.

Verse 18 further explains that the inheritance of salvation is not earned: it is given. Just as God gave it to Abraham, He freely gives it to us if we but believe. If, however, we choose to believe that our salvation comes by our works of righteousness, we ultimately believe that Christ's work on the cross was not sufficient for our salvation.

Galatians 2:21

21 I do not frustrate the grace of God: for if righteousness come by the law, then Christ is dead in vain.

II. The Reason for the Law

So if the covenant to Abraham could never be annulled or replaced, why did God give the law to Moses?

A. To Reveal Man's Need (vv. 19a, 21–22)

ROMANS 7:7–8

7 What shall we say then? Is the law sin? God forbid. Nay, I had not known sin, but by the law: for I had not known lust, except the law had said, Thou shalt not covet.

8 But sin, taking occasion by the commandment, wrought in me all manner of concupiscence. For without the law sin was dead.

ROMANS 4:15

15 Because the law worketh wrath: for where no law is, there is no transgression.

1. The law shows our transgression (v. 19a).

GALATIANS 3:24

24 Wherefore the law was our schoolmaster to bring us unto Christ, that we might be justified by faith.

ROMANS 3:20

20 Therefore by the deeds of the law there shall no flesh be justified in his sight: for by the law is the knowledge of sin.

2. The law could not give life (v. 21).

ROMANS 3:20–22

20 Therefore by the deeds of the law there shall no flesh be justified in his sight: for by the law is the knowledge of sin.

21 But now the righteousness of God without the law is manifested, being witnessed by the law and the prophets;

22 Even the righteousness of God which is by faith of Jesus Christ unto all and upon all them that believe: for there is no difference:

3. **The law condemns all men (v. 22a).**
    ROMANS 3:23
    23 For all have sinned, and come short of the glory of God;

B. **To Reveal the Superiority of Abraham's Covenant (vv. 19b—20)**

The Mosaic law was made between God and man with Moses as the mediator, but the Abraham Covenant was between God and Abraham alone.

The law was given by angelic mediators, but God spoke personally to Abraham. God is one being, and the fulfillment of His promise to Abraham depended on Him alone.

Therefore, the law was a temporary necessity until Jesus, the promised "Seed," came. Its purpose now is to teach us what sin is so we will see our need for a Saviour.

III. The Reception of Salvation (vv. 22- 25)

The law then, does not hinder the promise; it enhances the need for the promised gift of salvation to those who believe in Jesus Christ.

A. **The Provision of Salvation (v. 22)**
ROMANS 3:21–22
21 But now the righteousness of God without the law is manifested, being witnessed by the law and the prophets;
22 Even the righteousness of God which is by faith of Jesus Christ unto all and upon all them that believe: for there is no difference:

ROMANS 5:1
1 Therefore being justified by faith, we have peace with God through our Lord Jesus Christ.

B. The Provision of Justification (vv. 24–25)

The law was a prison for man. The word *kept* (v. 23) in Greek is *phroureo*, meaning "to guard, protect by a military guard."

In verse 24, the law is also called a schoolmaster. In other words, it shows us where we fall short, hence pointing us to Jesus!

Conclusion

Once we place our faith in Christ, there is no need for a guardian or a schoolmaster. We can come face to face with God through Christ.

Romans 6:14

14 *For sin shall not have dominion over you: for ye are not under the law, but under grace.*

Hebrews 10:15–18

15 *Whereof the Holy Ghost also is a witness to us: for after that he had said before,*
16 *This is the covenant that I will make with them after those days, saith the Lord, I will put my laws into their hearts, and in their minds will I write them;*
17 *And their sins and iniquities will I remember no more.*
18 *Now where remission of these is, there is no more offering for sin.*

OUTLINE TEN

THE FAMILY OF GOD
GALATIANS 3:26–29

26 For ye are all the children of God by faith in Christ Jesus.
27 For as many of you as have been baptized into Christ have put on Christ.
28 There is neither Jew nor Greek, there is neither bond nor free, there is neither male nor female: for ye are all one in Christ Jesus.
29 And if ye be Christ's, then are ye Abraham's seed, and heirs according to the promise.

Introduction
Depending on your experiences, thinking of family can either be comforting or emotional. Regardless of the quality of our relationships with our earthly family, we can always be thankful for our inheritance in Christ and that we are in God's family.

I. Invited to a Family (v. 26)

A. *God is the Father of All Creation*
1 CORINTHIANS 8:6

6 But to us there is but one God, the Father, of whom are all things, and we in him; and one Lord Jesus Christ, by whom are all things, and we by him.

Note—He is not the Father of all people redemptively.

B. *God is the Spiritual Father of the Saved (v. 26)*

1. **Before Christ, we are children of wrath.**
   EPHESIANS 2:3

   3 Among whom also we all had our conversation in times past in the lusts of our flesh, fulfilling the desires of the flesh and of the mind; and were by nature the children of wrath, even as others.

2. **Through Christ, we are the children of God.**
   JOHN 14:6

   6 Jesus saith unto him, I am the way, the truth, and the life: no man cometh unto the Father, but by me.

   A person who has not trusted Christ is not a child of God. God has no sons who are not identified by faith with His only Son, Christ Jesus. No one comes to the Father except through His Son

   JOHN 1:12

   12 But as many as received him, to them gave he power to become the sons of God, even to them that believe on his name:

3. **By the Holy Spirit, we are adopted children.**
   GALATIANS 4:6

   6 And because ye are sons, God hath sent forth the Spirit of his Son into your hearts, crying, Abba, Father.

Romans 8:16

16 *The Spirit itself beareth witness with our spirit, that we are the children of God:*

II. Identified with a Saviour (vv. 27–28)

In verses 27–28, Paul is not speaking primarily of water baptism because water baptism does not put us into Christ. He is speaking of our faith that has placed us in this position.

A. *In His Position (v. 27)*

The phrase *put on Christ* refers to a change of garments. The believer has laid aside the dirty garments of sin (Isaiah 64:6) and, by faith, received the robes of righteousness in Christ (Colossians 3:8–15).

Isaiah 64:6

6 *But we are all as an unclean thing, and all our righteousnesses are as filthy rags; and we all do fade as a leaf; and our iniquities, like the wind, have taken us away.*

Colossians 3:8–15

8 *But now ye also put off all these; anger, wrath, malice, blasphemy, filthy communication out of your mouth.*

9 *Lie not one to another, seeing that ye have put off the old man with his deeds;*

10 *And have put on the new man, which is renewed in knowledge after the image of him that created him:*

11 *Where there is neither Greek nor Jew, circumcision nor uncircumcision, Barbarian, Scythian, bond nor free: but Christ is all, and in all.*

12 *Put on therefore, as the elect of God, holy and beloved, bowels of mercies, kindness, humbleness of mind, meekness, longsuffering;*

13 *Forbearing one another, and forgiving one another, if any man have a quarrel against any: even as Christ forgave you, so also do ye.*

14 *And above all these things put on charity, which is the bond of perfectness.*

15 *And let the peace of God rule in your hearts, to the which also ye are called in one body; and be ye thankful.*

Note—The phrase *put on* in Greek is *enduo*, meaning "to sink into (clothing), put on, clothe one's self." To "put on" something means sink into it. When we "put on" Christ, the way we live is filtered through Him.

Galatians 2:20

20 *I am crucified with Christ: nevertheless I live; yet not I, but Christ liveth in me: and the life which I now live in the flesh I live by the faith of the Son of God, who loved me, and gave himself for me.*

B. In Our Practice

Because we are in Christ, we put on Christ.

Illustration— Someone who puts on an Army uniform isn't necessarily in the Army just because of the uniform. But someone who is in the Army does put on the Army uniform because he is in the Army.

Note—"To put on" is a middle voice, meaning that the action is being performed by the person upon himself. The putting on of a coat may be done by the person himself. So we are to "put on Christ." This is something we are to actively do.

Putting on Christ requires that we separate from worldliness.

Philippians 2:15

15 *That ye may be blameless and harmless, the sons of God, without rebuke, in the midst of a crooked and perverse nation, among whom ye shine as lights in the world;*

Romans 13:11–14

11 And that, knowing the time, that now it is high time to awake out of sleep: for now is our salvation nearer than when we believed.

12 The night is far spent, the day is at hand: let us therefore cast off the works of darkness, and let us put on the armour of light.

13 Let us walk honestly, as in the day; not in rioting and drunkenness, not in chambering and wantonness, not in strife and envying.

14 But put ye on the Lord Jesus Christ, and make not provision for the flesh, to fulfil the lusts thereof.

III. Included in the Promise (v. 29)

A. *The Promise Concerning Christ*

"Abraham's seed" in verse 29 is referring to Christ. The phrase "and if ye be Christ's" follows what Paul said at the end of verse 28, "…for ye are all one in Christ Jesus." This sums up the common position we have in Christ whether Jew or Gentile.

B. *The Promise For all People*

All believers, without exception, are one in Christ Jesus. All spiritual blessings, resources, and promises are equally given to all who believe unto salvation.

Romans 10:12

12 For there is no difference between the Jew and the Greek: for the same Lord over all is rich unto all that call upon him.

"Abraham's seed" refers back to verse 14, where it says that the blessing of Abraham came to the Gentiles as promised in the last part of the Abrahamic covenant.

Genesis 12:3

3 …And in thee shall all families of the earth be blessed.

As verse 14 says, this promise was fulfilled "through Jesus Christ." The end of verse 14 tells us that the purpose of this was so the Gentiles would receive "the promise of the Spirit through faith."

Conclusion

Our Christian lives ought to take on new wonder and meaning as we realize all that we have in Christ, and that all of it is by grace, not by keeping the law. We are sons and daughters in God's family, heirs of God. Are we drawing on our inheritance?

OUTLINE ELEVEN

CHILDREN OF GOD THROUGH CHRIST
GALATIANS 4:1–7

1 *Now I say, That the heir, as long as he is a child, differeth nothing from a servant, though he be lord of all;*
2 *But is under tutors and governors until the time appointed of the father.*
3 *Even so we, when we were children, were in bondage under the elements of the world:*
4 *But when the fulness of the time was come, God sent forth his Son, made of a woman, made under the law,*
5 *To redeem them that were under the law, that we might receive the adoption of sons.*
6 *And because ye are sons, God hath sent forth the Spirit of his Son into your hearts, crying, Abba, Father.*
7 *Wherefore thou art no more a servant, but a son; and if a son, then an heir of God through Christ.*

Introduction

One of the great truths of our study thus far is Galatians 3:26, "For ye are all the children of God by faith in Christ Jesus." Having stated the truth, the Apostle Paul now expands the truth. What does it mean to be the children of God? In these verses, he provides three answers.

I. Our Position as Heirs (vv. 1–3)

A. A Right to Future Inheritance (vv. 1-2, 7)

As long as an heir is a minor, he has no control over his inheritance, even though he will be lord of it all one day. But the heir would have the love of his father, the future promise of owning property.

EPHESIANS 2:13

13 *But now in Christ Jesus ye who sometimes were far off are made nigh by the blood of Christ.*

EPHESIANS 2:18

18 *For through him we both have access by one Spirit unto the Father.*

B. A Responsibility to Past Traditions (vv. 2- 3)

In verse 2, we see the son under teachers and governors until the father appoints his time to take responsibility and receive the possessions as his adult son. This metaphor refers to the spiritual condition before the Galatians were saved.

Note—Jews and Gentiles used to go by rules and regulations; and these kept us shut up, hemmed in, boxed in, and cut off from justification.

II. Our Pardon through Christ (vv. 4–5)

A. Made in His Time (v. 4a)

Our pardon came when time was marked by God for the moment for Christ to come. God waited until the time when all things were made ready for His coming.

B. Made in His Way (vv. 4b-5)

1. **Through redemption (v. 4b)**
   Christ was made of a woman and made under the law, yet He was perfect in keeping and then in fulfilling the law. Thus the source of our sonship is the true Son, Jesus Christ.

   EPHESIANS 1:7
   7 In whom we have redemption through his blood, the forgiveness of sins, according to the riches of his grace;

2. **Through adoption (v. 5b)**
   The word *adoption* in Greek is *huiothesia*, and is made up of the words "son" and "to place."

   According to Scripture, we become the sons of God the moment of our salvation. The Holy Spirit places the children of God as adult sons in a legal standing before God and in relation to Him. Thus, our adoption has to do with the end result of our salvation.

III. Our Provision as Sons (vv. 6–7)

Being a son in God's family makes valuable provisions available to us.

A. The Comfort of the Spirit (v. 6)
Because we are God's sons now, He gives us His Spirit to comfort us.

ROMANS 8:15–16
15 For ye have not received the spirit of bondage again to fear; but ye have received the Spirit of adoption, whereby we cry, Abba, Father.
16 The Spirit itself beareth witness with our spirit, that we are the children of God:

Ephesians 1:13–14

13 In whom ye also trusted, after that ye heard the word of truth, the gospel of your salvation: in whom also after that ye believed, ye were sealed with that holy Spirit of promise,

14 Which is the earnest of our inheritance until the redemption of the purchased possession, unto the praise of his glory.

B. The Covenant of Sonship (v. 7)

The covenant goes back to the first three verses. Paul explains that we are now not children, but rather adult sons who therefore receive the fullness of their inheritances. This inheritance is what we are waiting for.

Romans 8:17

17 And if children, then heirs; heirs of God, and joint-heirs with Christ; if so be that we suffer with him, that we may be also glorified together.

The earnest of the Spirit was God's promise to his sons that we would one day receive the fullness of our inheritance when we receive the adoption of sons at our glorification.

Conclusion

Thank God we are adopted as his sons! The adoption process carries with it a special meaning: when a child is adopted, he is chosen specifically to be a son to a father. God has chosen us all to be His sons. The process by which He did this was unlike any other. He gave His own biological Son, His flesh and blood to be a sacrifice so that we could be called His adopted sons. He is not willing that any of us should perish but rather that we receive the inheritance of Heaven one day and His Spirit even today.

OUTLINE TWELVE

BACK TO THE BLESSED PLACE
GALATIANS 4:8–15

8 *Howbeit then, when ye knew not God, ye did service unto them which by nature are no gods.*
9 *But now, after that ye have known God, or rather are known of God, how turn ye again to the weak and beggarly elements, whereunto ye desire again to be in bondage?*
10 *Ye observe days, and months, and times, and years.*
11 *I am afraid of you, lest I have bestowed upon you labour in vain.*
12 *Brethren, I beseech you, be as I am; for I am as ye are: ye have not injured me at all.*
13 *Ye know how through infirmity of the flesh I preached the gospel unto you at the first.*
14 *And my temptation which was in my flesh ye despised not, nor rejected; but received me as an angel of God, even as Christ Jesus.*
15 *Where is then the blessedness ye spake of? for I bear you record, that, if it had been possible, ye would have plucked out your own eyes, and have given them to me.*

Introduction

Before their salvation, the Galatians *were* religious (worshiping Dianna, Jupiter, and other gods), but they were also lost.

Paganism abounds in our day, and it's not just in remote jungle regions of the world. Consider the following examples.

Many dioceses today ordain openly gay men and women; in some, same-sex unions are celebrated.

The Episcopal Church ordains women to the priesthood as well as the diaconate and the episcopate. The current Presiding Bishop of the Episcopal Church is Katharine Jefferts Schori, the first female primate (bishop) in the Anglican Communion.

In 2009, at the inaugural concert given by Bruce Springsteen, Beyonce, and the Washington Gay Men's Chorus, Bishop Gene Robinson, the openly-homosexual Episcopal Bishop of New Hampshire, opened the mass event at the Lincoln Memorial with prayer. The New York Times reported this: "Bishop Robinson said he had been reading inaugural prayers through history and was 'horrified' at how 'specifically and aggressively Christian they were.' 'I am very clear,' he said, 'that this will not be a Christian prayer, and I won't be quoting Scripture or anything like that. The texts that I hold as sacred are not sacred texts for all Americans, and I want all people to feel that this is their prayer.' Bishop Robinson said he might address the prayer to 'the God of our many understandings,' language that he said he learned from the twelve-step program he attended for his alcohol addiction."

In many ways, paganism in our day is the same as it was in Paul's. Pagan Rome had a building called the Pantheon, which was for "all the gods." Polytheism is as prevalent today as it was in pagan Rome.

2 Timothy 3:5
5 *Having a form of godliness, but denying the power thereof: from such turn away.*

Quote—Religion today is not transforming the people—it is being transformed by the people. It is not raising the moral level of society—it is descending to society's own level and congratulating itself that it has scored a victory because society is smiling accepting its surrender. —A.W. Tozer

The Galatians had been saved from paganism, but now they were reverting to another form of religious bondage—Judaism. Paul points out the error to them and urges them to return to the place of spiritual blessing when they had joy in resting by faith in Christ.

I. The Relapse of the Galatians (vv. 8–10)

A. *The Record before Conversion (v. 8)*

1. They were religious.

Everyone on earth has a religious nature. Some worship the true God. Some worship Mohammad. Some worship Buddha. Some worship the thousands of gods in the Hindu religion. And some just worship themselves (Humanism).

The religious nature of people is to get caught up in works (what they do to perform their religion). The Galatians were no different. Before their salvation, their works defined how they worshiped their gods. In these verses, Paul addresses the fact that Judaism did the same thing as their pagan religions did—focused solely on their works.

2. They were idolaters.

During this period, many of the Romans, Greeks, and those who were influenced by their religious beliefs were also idolaters.

ROMANS 1:21–23

21 *Because that, when they knew God, they glorified him not as God, neither were thankful; but became*

vain in their imaginations, and their foolish heart was darkened.
22 Professing themselves to be wise, they became fools,
23 And changed the glory of the uncorruptible God into an image made like to corruptible man, and to birds, and fourfooted beasts, and creeping things.

B. The Record of Their Conversion (v. 9a)

"But now" the Galatians not only know God, but "rather" (to a greater degree, rather, much, by far), God knows them. This is quite a contrast to what God says about the lost.

2 Timothy 2:19
19 Nevertheless the foundation of God standeth sure, having this seal, The Lord knoweth them that are his. And, Let every one that nameth the name of Christ depart from iniquity.

Quote—Remember that if you are a child of God, you will never be happy in sin. You are spoiled for the world, the flesh, and the devil. When you were regenerated there was put into you a vital principle, which can never be content to dwell in the dead world. You will have to come back, if indeed you belong to the family.—C.H. Spurgeon

The Galatians had a sincere belief in their pagan religion, but they did not have Christ. Now these Galatians had been purchased by the blood of Christ and had become partakers of the divine nature.

2 Peter 1:3–4
3 According as his divine power hath given unto us all things that pertain unto life and godliness, through the knowledge of him that hath called us to glory and virtue:
4 Whereby are given unto us exceeding great and precious promises: that by these ye might be partakers of the divine nature, having escaped the corruption that is in the world through lust.

C. **The Relapse after Conversion (vv. 9b-10)**
   1. **They were turning back to bondage (v. 9).**
      Paul uses the words "how turn ye" to question how the Galatians would turn back from the freedom that Christ gave them by grace into a weak and beggarly system of works.

      Quote—If you are not as close to God as you used to be, you do not have to guess who moved.—Author Unknown

      The word *weak* in the Greek is *asthenes*, meaning, "weak, infirm, feeble." Paul is questioning the Galatians' choice after being set free from the bondage. Why would they go back to something that was weaker, feeble, and incapable of giving them peace and freedom?

      Paul uses the word *beggarly* in verse 9. In the Greek, *beggarly* is *ptochos* meaning, "lacking in anything—as respects their spirit." The Galatians were going back to a beggarly lifestyle if they placed themselves under works-based rituals.

   2. **They were turning back to rituals (v. 10).**
      The object of this verse was to specify what the Galatians had enslaved themselves to—the observing of Jewish days, months, times, and years.

      - Days: the weekly observance of the Sabbath
      - Months: the festivals of the new moon, kept by the Jews. On this festival, in addition to the daily sacrifice, two bullocks, a ram, and seven sheep of a year old were offered in sacrifice. The appearance of the new-moon was announced by the sound of trumpets

      NUMBERS 10:10
      10 Also in the day of your gladness, and in your solemn days, and in the beginnings of your months, ye shall

> *blow with the trumpets over your burnt offerings, and over the sacrifices of your peace offerings; that they may be to you for a memorial before your God: I am the LORD your God.*

- Times: festivals returning periodically, as the Passover, the Feast of Pentecost, and the Feast of Tabernacles.
- Years: the sabbatical year, or the year of jubilee.

What the Galatians had forsaken in paganism, they now were embracing in the legalism of Judaism. All they were doing was going from one form of slavery to another. They had been set free by the gospel from their bitter bondage of paganism. Now they had placed themselves into ritualistic bondage to the Jewish law and customs, leaving the freedom found in the gospel of Jesus Christ.

COLOSSIANS 2:13–14
> 13 *And you, being dead in your sins and the uncircumcision of your flesh, hath he quickened together with him, having forgiven you all trespasses;*
> 14 *Blotting out the handwriting of ordinances that was against us, which was contrary to us, and took it out of the way, nailing it to his cross;*

II. The Regret of the Apostle (v. 11)

A. *Paul's Fear for Their Faith*

Paul feared that he had preached the gospel in vain because the Galatians were wavering in the faith. This did not mean that they had lost their salvation, but they had lost the principles that salvation had given to them to live in their faith.

2 CORINTHIANS 11:2–3
> 2 *For I am jealous over you with godly jealousy: for I have espoused you to one husband, that I may present you as a chaste virgin to Christ.*

> 3 But I fear, lest by any means, as the serpent beguiled Eve through his subtilty, so your minds should be corrupted from the simplicity that is in Christ.

B. Paul's Fear of Their Failure

Paul feared that he had bestowed much labor into the Galatians, and now it would be in vain if they went back into the religious rituals from which they had been saved.

Paul also feared that he had "bestowed upon them labour," meaning he had placed much wearisome labor into their lives now, only to see them so easily pulled away by these false teachers.

III. The Reminder from the Apostle (vv. 12–15)

Paul gave clear instructions to the Galatian churches on how they could return to the blessedness of their salvation.

A. Follow His Example (vv. 12–13)

When you think of it, it's incredible that Paul could transparently invite others to follow Christ by following him. This speaks of the genuineness of Paul's walk with God.

Specifically, he encouraged them to follow his example in two areas.

1. In living (v. 12)

In this verse, Paul emphasizes the importance of our testimony.

MATTHEW 4:19

> 19 And he saith unto them, Follow me, and I will make you fishers of men.

1 CORINTHIANS 11:1

> 1 Be ye followers of me, even as I also am of Christ.

2. **In preaching (v. 13)**

   1 Corinthians 2:3–5

   3 *And I was with you in weakness, and in fear, and in much trembling.*

   4 *And my speech and my preaching was not with enticing words of man's wisdom, but in demonstration of the Spirit and of power:*

   5 *That your faith should not stand in the wisdom of men, but in the power of God.*

B. Remember Their Love (vv. 14–15)

A similar exhortation to remember and return to love for Christ was later given to the Ephesian church.

Revelation 2:4–5

4 *Nevertheless I have somewhat against thee, because thou hast left thy first love.*

5 *Remember therefore from whence thou art fallen, and repent, and do the first works; or else I will come unto thee quickly, and will remove thy candlestick out of his place, except thou repent.*

When Paul had first come to Galatia preaching the gospel, the people had received Paul's message even with his infirmity (v. 14). In fact, at that time they had such compassion for Paul that they were willing to go to any length—even if it meant plucking out their own eyes for him—to convey their love and help him (v. 15). But now the Galatians had forgotten the love they had for the Apostle Paul and for his message.

Conclusion

God calls out to his backslidden children because He loves them! Jesus illustrated this with Thomas after he doubted Christ's resurrection. Thomas answered Him with a humble, "My Lord and my God!" Only a God of love would come back for a doubter. Desert God—He'll still love you. Deny God—He'll still love you. Doubt God—He'll still love you.

OUTLINE THIRTEEN

STAYING ON THE RIGHT PATH
GALATIANS 4:16–31

16 Am I therefore become your enemy, because I tell you the truth?
17 They zealously affect you, but not well; yea, they would exclude you, that ye might affect them.
18 But it is good to be zealously affected always in a good thing, and not only when I am present with you.
19 My little children, of whom I travail in birth again until Christ be formed in you,
20 I desire to be present with you now, and to change my voice; for I stand in doubt of you.
21 Tell me, ye that desire to be under the law, do ye not hear the law?
22 For it is written, that Abraham had two sons, the one by a bondmaid, the other by a freewoman.
23 But he who was of the bondwoman was born after the flesh; but he of the freewoman was by promise.
24 Which things are an allegory: for these are the two covenants; the one from the mount Sinai, which gendereth to bondage, which is Agar.

25 *For this Agar is mount Sinai in Arabia, and answereth to Jerusalem which now is, and is in bondage with her children.*
26 *But Jerusalem which is above is free, which is the mother of us all.*
27 *For it is written, Rejoice, thou barren that bearest not; break forth and cry, thou that travailest not: for the desolate hath many more children than she which hath an husband.*
28 *Now we, brethren, as Isaac was, are the children of promise.*
29 *But as then he that was born after the flesh persecuted him that was born after the Spirit, even so it is now.*
30 *Nevertheless what saith the scripture? Cast out the bondwoman and her son: for the son of the bondwoman shall not be heir with the son of the freewoman.*
31 *So then, brethren, we are not children of the bondwoman, but of the free.*

Introduction

Thus far in Galatians, the Apostle Paul has been challenging the church of Galatia back to the blessedness of their first love. Each of us must be challenged to stay in love with the Lord and serve Him from a heart of grace and gratitude. In this passage, Paul reminds his readers that to stay in love with the Lord, they must separate from the world and keep perspective of what Christ did for them.

I. The Problem of a Fleshly Influence (vv. 16–21)

The influence of the Judaizers was affecting the Galatian believers in three specific ways.

A. Misrepresentation of the Apostle (v. 16)

1. **False teachers had maligned Paul.**
   Only enemies of truth are to be known as our enemies.

   JAMES 4:4
   4 *Ye adulterers and adulteresses, know ye not that the friendship of the world is enmity with God? whosoever*

therefore will be a friend of the world is the enemy of God.

2. **Paul had been faithful to the truth.**
   Paul's purpose in preaching the truth of the gospel was to keep the message of salvation pure for all people. While this message may have offended some of the Galatian believers, Paul remained faithful to the truth.

   GALATIANS 1:10
   10 For do I now persuade men, or God? or do I seek to please men? for if I yet pleased men, I should not be the servant of Christ.

   PROVERBS 27:6
   6 Faithful are the wounds of a friend; but the kisses of an enemy are deceitful.

B. *Manipulation of New Christians (v. 17)*
   True to the nature of false teachers, these Judaizers specifically targeted young Christians.

   1. **False teachers pursue new believers (v.17a).**
      The word *affect* in the Greek is *zeloo*, meaning, "to desire earnestly, pursue; to desire one earnestly, to strive after." The false teachers earnestly pursued after the young Galatian believers in order to persuade them from the truth.

   2. **False teachers pull believers away (v. 17b).**
      The word *exclude* in the Greek is *ekkleio*, meaning, "to shut out, to turn out of doors; to prevent the approach of one."

      The tactic of false teachers is to separate the new believers from the congregation by their false teachings. The false teachers were zealous in their efforts to get these believers back under the law. When the Galatians showed some response to their efforts, the false teachers became more enthusiastic.

In Paul's day the false teachers were the Judaizers. Today it may be Mormons, Jehovah Witnesses, Charismatics, or others. It is always someone who says they have more knowledge and understanding to add to Bible faith.

Quote—It is a remarkable fact that all the heresies which have arisen in the Christian Church have had a decided tendency to dishonor God and to flatter man. —C.H. Spurgeon

1 Corinthians 4:14–15
14 I write not these things to shame you, but as my beloved sons I warn you.
15 For though ye have ten thousand instructors in Christ, yet have ye not many fathers: for in Christ Jesus I have begotten you through the gospel.

Romans 16:17–18
17 Now I beseech you, brethren, mark them which cause divisions and offences contrary to the doctrine which ye have learned; and avoid them.
18 For they that are such serve not our Lord Jesus Christ, but their own belly; and by good words and fair speeches deceive the hearts of the simple.

Quote—The early Christians condemned false doctrine in a way that sounds almost unchristian today. —Vance Havner

C. Misplaced Zeal (v. 18–21)
Paul was not opposed to a new believer having zeal for understanding, for serving, and for seeking God. But Paul

qualifies his statement by making it clear they should have a zeal for what is good.

In verse 19, the phrase *my little children* in Greek is *teknia*, meaning, "little child—an infant to primary age." This term indicates what the maturity level is of the Galatians. The Galatians had zeal but no maturity (vv. 19–21).

The word *formed* in the Greek is *morphoo*, meaning, "to form." Paul explains in this verse that until the Galatians were molded after the image of Christ, he would continue to work with them toward maturity.

ROMANS 8:28–29
28 And we know that all things work together for good to them that love God, to them who are the called according to his purpose.

29 For whom he did foreknow, he also did predestinate to be conformed to the image of his Son, that he might be the firstborn among many brethren.

This growth process was interrupted by the Judaizers coming among them and confusing them with their false teachings.

In verse 21, Paul uses the phrase "stand in doubt." This phrase in the Greek is *aporeo*, meaning, "to be in doubt, not to know how to decide or what to do, to be perplexed." Paul is perplexed at their turn toward the false teaching and how easily perhaps they were being persuaded.

II. The Picture of Law and Grace (vv. 22–27)

Here, Paul directly confronts the teaching of the Judaizers as he deals with an Old Testament picture of the law and grace.

A. *The Sons of Abraham*

Paul uses the two sons of Abraham to contrast the law and grace.

1. **The flesh versus faith (vv. 22–23)**

    a. *The son of the flesh—Ishmael*
    Ishmael was "born after the flesh" to Abraham by Hagar, an Egyptian bondslave, Sarah's handmaid.

    GENESIS 16:15
    15 *And Hagar bare Abram a son: and Abram called his son's name, which Hagar bare, Ishmael.*

    Ishmael was born because Sarah had lost faith and gave Hagar to Abraham in order to produce an heir.

    Whatever is not done in faith is done through the flesh and is not of God's work.

    ROMANS 14:23
    23 *And he that doubteth is damned if he eat, because he eateth not of faith: for whatsoever is not of faith is sin.*

    The fleshly child (Ishmael) was born of the bondwoman. The Galatians going back into the law and trying to live by the law in the strength of their flesh, would put them under bondage once again.

    b. *The son of faith—Isaac*
    Isaac was born of Sarah, a free woman according to the promises God gave to Abraham.

    GENESIS 21:1–2
    1 *And the LORD visited Sarah as he had said, and the LORD did unto Sarah as he had spoken.*
    2 *For Sarah conceived, and bare Abraham a son in his old age, at the set time of which God had spoken to him.*

    When Abraham and Sarah believed God, they received the promised son. Faith is based on God's Word and His integrity to keep His promises.

At age eighty-six, Abraham had a son in the flesh. Years later, Abraham (one hundred years old) and Sarah (ninety years old) gave birth to the heir of promise. God did this miracle in His power, not through man's.

2. **The Law versus grace (vv. 24–27)**
Hagar, Sarah's bondwoman, represents the law, for she was held under bondage and required to do the works of her master.

At Mt. Sinai God gave a conditional covenant that said if the children of Israel obeyed the law, He would bless them (v. 25).

In Paul's day, the Jews who lived in Jerusalem, who had rejected the gospel concerning Jesus Christ, were like Hagar.

JAMES 2:10

10 *For whosoever shall keep the whole law, and yet offend in one point, he is guilty of all.*

GALATIANS 3:10

10 *For as many as are of the works of the law are under the curse: for it is written, Cursed is every one that continueth not in all things which are written in the book of the law to do them.*

Unlike Hagar, Sarah represents grace, for she was free to follow God by faith. This is a picture of the freedom we have from sin to serve God.

B. *The Gospel's Freedom (vv. 26–27)*
In verse 26, the direction is turned toward the spiritual (heavenly) Jerusalem. We see two results for those who are saved:

- They are set free from the bondage of sin, death, and the law's condemnation.
- The gospel will produce fruit of the barren (Sarah) that the law (Hagar) could not produce.

Rather than being bound to the law for our salvation, we are freed from the law by grace to serve God.

III. The Path of the Spiritually Free (vv. 28–31)

A. We Are Born into the Promise (v. 28).

Through being born again, we become the children of promise, and because we are God's children, He promises us the benefits of salvation.

1 John 3:1–2

1 Behold, what manner of love the Father hath bestowed upon us, that we should be called the sons of God: therefore the world knoweth us not, because it knew him not.

2 Beloved, now are we the sons of God, and it doth not yet appear what we shall be: but we know that, when he shall appear, we shall be like him; for we shall see him as he is.

B. We Are Subject to Persecution and Trials (v. 29).

Just as Ishmael made fun of Isaac and mocked him, so the believers in Paul's day were being criticized and persecuted.

Genesis 21:9

9 And Sarah saw the son of Hagar the Egyptian, which she had born unto Abraham, mocking.

Romans 11:28

28 As concerning the gospel, they are enemies for your sakes: but as touching the election, they are beloved for the fathers' sakes.

C. We Must Separate from False Teaching (vv. 30–31).

Just as the bondwoman's son could not remain in the same household as the promised heir, Judaizers could not fellowship with the church of Galatia.

GENESIS 21:10

10 *Wherefore she said unto Abraham, Cast out this bondwoman and her son: for the son of this bondwoman shall not be heir with my son, even with Isaac.*

ROMANS 8:15–18

15 *For ye have not received the spirit of bondage again to fear; but ye have received the Spirit of adoption, whereby we cry, Abba, Father.*

16 *The Spirit itself beareth witness with our spirit, that we are the children of God:*

17 *And if children, then heirs; heirs of God, and joint-heirs with Christ; if so be that we suffer with him, that we may be also glorified together.*

18 *For I reckon that the sufferings of this present time are not worthy to be compared with the glory which shall be revealed in us.*

Conclusion

Like the Galatians, we will always be pulled from our growth in grace by fleshly influences, manifested in two possible directions: licentious, ungodly living and a legalistic spirit of earning God's favor by keeping the law. The answer for us today is the same as it was for the Galatians in Paul's day. We must separate ourselves from false teachers. We must not allow false teachers to infiltrate our churches and persuade our young believers. And like Paul, we must be conscious of strengthening immature believers until they are molded after the image of Christ.

OUTLINE FOURTEEN

Until Christ Be Formed in You
Galatians 4:19–20

19 *My little children, of whom I travail in birth again until Christ be formed in you,*
20 *I desire to be present with you now, and to change my voice; for I stand in doubt of you.*

2 Corinthians 3:2
2 *Ye are our epistle written in our hearts, known and read of all men:*

Introduction

In our previous outline we saw Paul's challenge to the Galatians to stay on the right path. In this outline, we will take a closer look at two verses from the previous text. These two verses give a glimpse into the heart of the Apostle Paul and his care for the spiritual development of each of these Christians.

2 Corinthians 3:2
2 *Ye are our epistle written in our hearts, known and read of all men:*

To the heart of a spiritual shepherd, nothing matters more than Christ being formed in those he leads. As an administrator, he will be interested in the various church ministries, the staff development, the finances, and hundreds of other details. But as a shepherd, his care is that each member of the church be growing in spiritual maturity.

Much of contemporary church ministry, while it may be successful in attracting a crowd, is failing in the goal of Christlikeness and developing the spiritual maturity that focuses on being conformed to the image of Christ.

Quote—The church needs people who, in listening to their pastor, listen for the message of Christ, and pastors who, in labouring among the people, look for the image of Christ.—John R. W. Stott

In these two verses, the Apostle Paul gives a ministry philosophy that centers on Christlikeness.

I. The Pattern for Ministry (v. 19b)

A. *A Christ Centered Pattern*

Note the words in verse 19, "until Christ..." Jesus Christ is the pattern for every believer to follow, and He is the model we strive for.

PHILIPPIANS 2:5–8

5 *Let this mind be in you, which was also in Christ Jesus:*

6 *Who, being in the form of God, thought it not robbery to be equal with God:*

7 *But made himself of no reputation, and took upon him the form of a servant, and was made in the likeness of men:*

8 *And being found in fashion as a man, he humbled himself, and became obedient unto death, even the death of the cross.*

1 PETER 2:21

21 *For even hereunto were ye called: because Christ also suffered for us, leaving us an example, that ye should follow his steps:*

The goal in ministry is never outward conformity; the goal is Jesus!

B. *A Christ Centered Purpose*

The phrase *be formed in you* is from the Greek word *morphoo* and means "to form, not to the external and transient, but to the inward—expressing the necessity of a change in character and conduct."

Paul is sharing that his heart for these believers is that they be conformed to the image of Christ from the inside out.

EPHESIANS 4:13–15

13 *Till we all come in the unity of the faith, and of the knowledge of the Son of God, unto a perfect man, unto the measure of the stature of the fulness of Christ:*

14 *That we henceforth be no more children, tossed to and fro, and carried about with every wind of doctrine, by the sleight of men, and cunning craftiness, whereby they lie in wait to deceive;*

15 *But speaking the truth in love, may grow up into him in all things, which is the head, even Christ:*

The pattern for ministry is never conformity to the leader; it is the development of Christlikeness from the heart.

II. The Process of Ministry (vv. 19–20)

Here we go back to the beginning of verse 19 and see the intensity of process involved in ministry.

In the Galatian churches, this process was being interrupted by the Judaizers.

Note—This process is what we call "ministry."

A. Personal Relationship

Disciples are made, not born. They require a personal, sacrificial relationship—much like that between a parent and a child.

1. **My children (v. 19a)**

    The word *children* refers to them as infants. Indeed, the Galatian believers *were* infants in Christ. What stands out here, however, is that Paul said, "I travail in birth again…." He is implying that while it is normal for a young Christian to need a spiritual parent, it is abnormal for a Christian to regress again to the point of salvation. The spiritual regression of these Christians was causing Paul to go through the intensity of spiritual labor as he did to first lead them to Christ.

    When we consider the personal relationship required for discipling young Christians, we are reminded of the pattern Christ set with His disciples.

    Jesus personally selected His disciples and chose to invest in their lives.

    MATTHEW 4:18–20
    18 And Jesus, walking by the sea of Galilee, saw two brethren, Simon called Peter, and Andrew his brother, casting a net into the sea: for they were fishers.
    19 And he saith unto them, Follow me, and I will make you fishers of men.
    20 And they straightway left their nets, and followed him.

    Additionally, Jesus spent time teaching His disciples privately.

    MATTHEW 16:13–15
    13 When Jesus came into the coasts of Caesarea Philippi, he asked his disciples, saying, Whom do men say that I the Son of man am?

> *14 And they said, Some say that thou art John the Baptist: some, Elias; and others, Jeremias, or one of the prophets.*
>
> *15 He saith unto them, But whom say ye that I am?*

Paul was also careful to invest in others. Specifically, we see his ongoing investment in Timothy.

> **1 Corinthians 16:10**
>
> *10 Now if Timotheus come, see that he may be with you without fear: for he worketh the work of the Lord, as I also do.*

2. **My desire (v. 20)**

   Personal relationships require personal time. Paul gave heavily of his time to the Galatian churches, and even now, he expressed his deep desire to be present with them.

   Note—There is great potential for the Internet and ministry, but nothing replaces the personal interaction of God's design of the local church.

   In the absence of physical proximity, Paul did not have a solid gauge for these believers. Thus, he said, "I stand in doubt of you." He knew they were struggling and that they had been corrupted by false doctrine, but he didn't know just how far their hearts had gone.

   There is no substitute for personal relationships in discipling ministry.

B. *Practical Labor (v. 19b)*

   The phrase "of whom I travail" sums up in four words the multi-faceted labor of pastoral ministry.

   1. **Travail in the Word**

> **2 Timothy 4:1–3**
> 1 *I charge thee therefore before God, and the Lord Jesus Christ, who shall judge the quick and the dead at his appearing and his kingdom;*
> 2 *Preach the word; be instant in season, out of season; reprove, rebuke, exhort with all longsuffering and doctrine.*
> 3 *For the time will come when they will not endure sound doctrine; but after their own lusts shall they heap to themselves teachers, having itching ears;*

New Testament pastoral ministry includes a true labor in study and preaching of the Word.

2. Travail in trials

> **1 Peter 1:6**
> 6 *Wherein ye greatly rejoice, though now for a season, if need be, ye are in heaviness through manifold temptations:*

There are always trials involved in ministry.

3. Travail in prayers

> **2 Timothy 1:3**
> 3 *I thank God, whom I serve from my forefathers with pure conscience, that without ceasing I have remembrance of thee in my prayers night and day;*

4. Travail in oversight

> **1 Peter 5:2**
> 2 *Feed the flock of God which is among you, taking the oversight thereof, not by constraint, but willingly; not for filthy lucre, but of a ready mind;*

In addition to preaching, praying, and continuing through personal and ministry trials, a pastor must maintain both spiritual and administrative oversight for the flock. This requires labor indeed.

III. The Product in Ministry (v. 19b)

How specifically is the pattern of Christlikeness developed through the process of personal relationships?

A. *Inward Molding*

This is the heart-level work of God. It is the process of the Holy Spirit developing a heart for God from within.

Hebrews 10:22

22 *Let us draw near with a true heart in full assurance of faith, having our hearts sprinkled from an evil conscience, and our bodies washed with pure water.*

Romans 8:29

29 *For whom he did foreknow, he also did predestinate to be conformed to the image of his Son, that he might be the firstborn among many brethren.*

Philippians 3:10–14

10 *That I may know him, and the power of his resurrection, and the fellowship of his sufferings, being made conformable unto his death;*

11 *If by any means I might attain unto the resurrection of the dead.*

12 *Not as though I had already attained, either were already perfect: but I follow after, if that I may apprehend that for which also I am apprehended of Christ Jesus.*

13 *Brethren, I count not myself to have apprehended: but this one thing I do, forgetting those things which are behind, and reaching forth unto those things which are before,*

14 *I press toward the mark for the prize of the high calling of God in Christ Jesus.*

B. **Outward Manifestation**
The inward molding will invariably show itself in an outward manifestation of Christlikeness.

Illustration—An overweight woman went to a diet center one day, and after being weighed in, she stood in front of a mirror while the person in charge outlined a shape several inches slimmer and explained, "Our goal is, at the end of ten weeks, to have you fit into this outline."

The woman worked hard. She dieted and exercised, and every week she came into the center and stood in front of the mirror. But she couldn't' quite fit into the outlined proportion. So she went home and worked even harder.

Then one day when she stood in front of the mirror, she was conformed to its image. (from *Come Walk with Me* by Carole Mayhall, Random House, 2010, 159.)

This anecdote illustrates the truth that God has a pre-designed shape—the image of Christ—toward which He is working to conform us. And He instructs us to partner with Him in the process.

ROMANS 12:2
2   *And be not conformed to this world: but be ye transformed by the renewing of your mind, that ye may prove what is that good, and acceptable, and perfect, will of God.*

The word *transformed* is from the Greek word *metamorphoo* which means, "to change into another form, to transform, to transfigure."

A Christian's life should be distinct both in his outward testimony and demeanor. The outside should reveal what God has been doing on the inside!

Conclusion

In the following chapter of Galatians, Paul details what Christlikeness looks like when he lists the fruits of the Spirit.

But one thing is certain here: the goal of ministry is being conformed to the image of Christ. Are you cooperating with the Holy Spirit toward Christ being formed in you? Are you travailing in labor for others that Christ would be formed in them?

OUTLINE FIFTEEN

STAND FAST
GALATIANS 5:1–6

1 Stand fast therefore in the liberty wherewith Christ hath made us free, and be not entangled again with the yoke of bondage.
2 Behold, I Paul say unto you, that if ye be circumcised, Christ shall profit you nothing.
3 For I testify again to every man that is circumcised, that he is a debtor to do the whole law.
4 Christ is become of no effect unto you, whosoever of you are justified by the law; ye are fallen from grace.
5 For we through the Spirit wait for the hope of righteousness by faith.
6 For in Jesus Christ neither circumcision availeth any thing, nor uncircumcision; but faith which worketh by love.

Introduction

Regarding the subject of doctrine, Galatians is a series of contrasts between the way of law and the way of grace, the way of works and the way of faith, the way of man and the way of God.

The Judaizers were persecuting the children of God. Interestingly, those who trust in God have always been persecuted by those who trust in themselves. True believers have always been more mistreated and oppressed by religionists than by atheists. It is the false religious system of Revelation 17:6 that is "drunk with the blood of the saints." But one day the persecutors will be thrown out, and the faithful will be blessed.

Paul has been defending justification by faith, but in this section, he is now going to give challenges to the Galatians for the practical Christian life.

There will be a constant pull from false teachers to abandon the truth and grace of Christ. Our response should be three-fold:

I. Stand in Christian Liberty (v. 1)

In Galatians 4:28–31, Paul showed how the bondwoman and her son were cast out and that the Galatian believers were not of the bondwoman but of the free woman. Now Paul challenges them to stand in that freedom.

The final two chapters of Galatians are a portrait of the Spirit-filled life, of the believer's implementing the life of faith under the control and in the energy of the Holy Spirit.

A. The Position of Our Stand (v. 1a)

The word *liberty* means "to be free." A believer's true liberty in Christ is when he has been released from bondage or slavery of sin and the law.

Through Christ, believers have liberty from sin and are completely accepted in Christ. This deliverance from sin and the law frees a believer to walk in the Spirit.

ROMANS 6:17–18

17 But God be thanked, that ye were the servants of sin, but ye have obeyed from the heart that form of doctrine which was delivered you.

18 *Being then made free from sin, ye became the servants of righteousness.*

Christ set us free from the guilt-establishing and deadening power of the law through His death and resurrection. The believers in Galatia were being duped by the Judaizers to consider returning to this same bondage.

B. *The Persistency of Our Stand (v. 1a)*

The phrase *stand fast* in Greek is *steko*, meaning, "to stand firm; to persevere, to persist; to keep one's standing." Paul is telling these Galatians to hold their ground.

EPHESIANS 6:11–13
11 *Put on the whole armour of God, that ye may be able to stand against the wiles of the devil.*
12 *For we wrestle not against flesh and blood, but against principalities, against powers, against the rulers of the darkness of this world, against spiritual wickedness in high places.*
13 *Wherefore take unto you the whole armour of God, that ye may be able to withstand in the evil day, and having done all, to stand.*

Repeatedly throughout Scripture, we are told to stand on our faith and beliefs.

1 CORINTHIANS 16:13
13 *Watch ye, stand fast in the faith, quit you like men, be strong.*

2 THESSALONIANS 2:15
15 *Therefore, brethren, stand fast, and hold the traditions which ye have been taught, whether by word, or our epistle.*

II. Stand against the Yoke of Bondage (vv. 2a–4)

A. *The Definition of Bondage (v. 2)*
Jews were often identified as "the circumcised."

Quote—Human legalism leads to human self-righteousness. Human self-righteousness denies the need for the saving, enabling grace of Christ. Human righteousness embraces the cruelest of Satan's lies, that a person can be righteous by keeping the law. If that were true, there would have been no need for the birth, life, death, and resurrection of Christ.
—Paul Tripp

B. The Debt of Bondage (vv. 3–4)

The word *testify* means, "to declare solemnly, protest." Paul is emphasizing again what the law was capable and incapable of doing.

- The law is capable of condemning.
- The law is incapable of saving.

ROMANS 8:3

3 For what the law could not do, in that it was weak through the flesh, God sending his own Son in the likeness of sinful flesh, and for sin, condemned sin in the flesh:

Those who had placed themselves under the law, made themselves indebted to perform and keep the *whole* law. Therefore, a man who became circumcised professed the Jewish religion and bound himself to obey all its laws. If he did it with a view for justification, or as a thing that was necessary and binding, then he essentially trusted in the works of the law, and was certain to fail.

GALATIANS 3:10

10 For as many as are of the works of the law are under the curse: for it is written, Cursed is every one that continueth not in all things which are written in the book of the law to do them.

C. The Danger of Bondage

Verse 4 tells us the final results if a man tried to keep the law in order to get or keep his salvation: "Christ is become *of no effect*," meaning, "to render idle, inactivate, inoperative." In other words, Christ's work for salvation is of no avail. This did not mean they lost their salvation, only that Christ's death was meaningless.

GALATIANS 2:21
21 *I do not frustrate the grace of God: for if righteousness come by the law, then Christ is dead in vain.*

III. Stay with the Hope of Salvation (vv. 5–6)

We stand against the yoke of bondage, but it is because we have something so much better—the hope of salvation. How do we stay with it?

A. Through the Spirit (v. 5)

The legalist is always filled with insecurity regarding his standing with God. However, we who know Christ wait "through the Spirit." We are sealed and confident.

ROMANS 8:10–11
10 *And if Christ be in you, the body is dead because of sin; but the Spirit is life because of righteousness.*
11 *But if the Spirit of him that raised up Jesus from the dead dwell in you, he that raised up Christ from the dead shall also quicken your mortal bodies by his Spirit that dwelleth in you.*

Illustration—A husband and wife didn't really love each other. The man was very demanding, so much so that he prepared a list of rules and regulations for his wife to follow. He insisted that she read them over every day and obey them to the letter. Among other things, his "do's and don'ts" indicated such details as what time she had to get up in the morning, when his breakfast should be served, and how the housework should be done. After several long years, the husband died.

As time passed, the woman fell in love with another man, one who dearly loved her. Soon they were married. This husband did everything he could to make his new wife happy, continually showering her with tokens of his appreciation. One day when she was cleaning house, she found tucked away in a drawer the list of commands her first husband had drawn up for her. As she looked it over, it dawned on her that even though her present husband hadn't given her any kind of list, she was doing everything her first husband's list required anyway. She realized she was so devoted to this man that her deepest desire was to please him out of love, not obligation.

This love relationship is an example of the way we respond to God through His Spirit. When we remember Christ's sacrifice for us and God's forgiveness to us, we walk in the Spirit and don't fulfill the lusts of flesh. (sermonillustrations.com)

B. Through Faith (v. 6)

The fruit of the Spirit is love. Our love is the result of justification by faith.

ROMANS 13:10

10 *Love worketh no ill to his neighbour: therefore love is the fulfilling of the law.*

Conclusion

Although the law condemns us, Christ forgave us. By keeping our perspective on Christ's sacrifice for us, we need no law to tell us how to stay in line. Instead, we can walk in Christian liberty in the Spirit and serve Christ because we want to serve Him, not because the law requires us to serve Him.

OUTLINE SIXTEEN

STAY IN THE RACE
GALATIANS 5:6–15

6 For in Jesus Christ neither circumcision availeth any thing, nor uncircumcision; but faith which worketh by love.
7 Ye did run well; who did hinder you that ye should not obey the truth?
8 This persuasion cometh not of him that calleth you.
9 A little leaven leaveneth the whole lump.
10 I have confidence in you through the Lord, that ye will be none otherwise minded: but he that troubleth you shall bear his judgment, whosoever he be.
11 And I, brethren, if I yet preach circumcision, why do I yet suffer persecution? then is the offence of the cross ceased.
12 I would they were even cut off which trouble you.
13 For, brethren, ye have been called unto liberty; only use not liberty for an occasion to the flesh, but by love serve one another.
14 For all the law is fulfilled in one word, even in this; Thou shalt love thy neighbour as thyself.
15 But if ye bite and devour one another, take heed that ye be not consumed one of another.

Introduction

Illustration—Olympic runner Bernard Lagat from Kenya was being interviewed and was asked why so many from his country were world class runners. He paused briefly and then suggested it may be the road signs in Africa: "Beware of Lions."

The Judaizers were trying to get the Galatian believers to quit the race. At times, even other Galatian believers became a hindrance to the church at Galatia. In this passage, Paul reminds the Galatians of the importance of staying in the race for the right reasons.

I. A False Persuasion

What was hindering the Galatians' spiritual progress? The problems were two-fold:

A. *A People Problem (vv. 6–8)*

1. **The people identified (v. 6)**
   The Judaizers were trying to persuade the Galatian Gentile believers that they had to follow the law which included circumcision. Paul contrasts this teaching by saying, "but faith which worketh by love."

   The word *worketh* in Greek is *energeo*, meaning, "to be operative, be at work, put forth power, to effect." The Christian life is to be lived by faith and motivated by love.

2. **The purpose inhibited (v. 7)**
   In verse 7, Paul asks a simple but convicting question: "Ye did run well; who did hinder you that ye should not obey the truth?"

   The word *run* in Greek is *trecho*, meaning, "to run; of those who run in a race course; by a metaphor taken from runners in a race, to exert one's self, strive hard." Before these false teachers came to the Galatians, they were doing well. Their Christian race was going well.

Paul uses the runner to illustrate how well the Galatians were doing. Then he asks what it was that hindered them.

The word *hinder* in Greek is *anakopto*, meaning, "to beat back, check (as in the course of a ship)." Here in the text, Paul paints a picture of a runner in a race who is distracted or beaten back by an obstacle or another runner. Paul's point is that the Galatian believers were doing well, but they needed to stop and think about why they were now being hindered in their growth.

1 Corinthians 9:24–27

24 Know ye not that they which run in a race run all, but one receiveth the prize? So run, that ye may obtain.

25 And every man that striveth for the mastery is temperate in all things. Now they do it to obtain a corruptible crown; but we an incorruptible.

26 I therefore so run, not as uncertainly; so fight I, not as one that beateth the air:

27 But I keep under my body, and bring it into subjection: lest that by any means, when I have preached to others, I myself should be a castaway.

In verse 8, Paul uses the word *persuasion*. The Greek word is *peismone*, meaning, "treacherous or deceptive persuasion." Paul is warning these young believers that what they had been persuaded by was not right or good, and definitely not from the one who called them into salvation and the Christian life.

Proverbs 1:10

10 My son, if sinners entice thee, consent thou not.

B. *A Portion Problem (v. 9)*

Leaven is yeast, and when added into bread dough it expands and spreads throughout the pile of dough. So it was with these false teachings: they affected the whole church family.

The proportion of this problem, if not stopped, had full potential to damage the whole church.

The Judaizers taught self-justification through circumcision, but would they stop there? They could have presented a multitude of laws for the Gentiles to follow:

- Adjusting their diet according to Leviticus 11
- Keeping all the feasts
- Following the laws of purification

Paul is saying that once yeast starts, it permeates the whole lump. And so it is with justifying oneself with the law. Once a believer starts, it spreads into every part of his life and influence.

II. A Firm Conviction (vv. 10–12)

Although the Galatians had been hindered in their spiritual progress, Paul had confidence that they would receive his warning and return to a life of grace.

A. *The Choice of the Galatians (v. 10)*

The word *confidence* means, "the feeling or belief that one can rely on someone or something; firm trust; the state of feeling certain about the truth of something."

Paul's confidence, or being convinced, that the Galatians would not be further persuaded was from the Lord.

2 THESSALONIANS 3:4
4   And we have confidence in the Lord touching you, that ye both do and will do the things which we command you.

B. *The Offense of the Cross (v. 11)*

Paul gave two examples to point to the supremacy and sufficiency of the cross of Christ.

First, he pointed out that if he were still preaching circumcision, as he did before he was converted, then why was he being persecuted for his message and life?

1 Corinthians 15:30
30 And why stand we in jeopardy every hour?

The obvious answer was that he was *not* preaching circumcision.

Paul was persecuted, as the Galatian churches would have known. He had been stoned on his first missionary journey, during which he established churches in Galatia. In fact, he had been persecuted by the very ones who were bothering the Galatians at the present time.

Paul's second example was that if the cross was no longer offensive, then it wouldn't still be under attack. But the cross was offensive and attacked because it spoke of grace not law, and "done" not "do."

III. A Faithful Mission (vv. 13–15)

There was a distinct reason Paul wanted the Galatians to stay in the race, and that was to fulfill their God-given mission to live and serve in the liberty of grace.

A. A Calling (v. 13)

Through salvation, we are called to a life of liberty. This liberty, of course, is not to be used for occasion for the flesh.

The word *occasion* is derived from two Greek words, *aphorme*, meaning, "a place from which a movement or attack is made, a base of operations" and *metaph*, meaning, "that by which endeavour is excited and from which it goes forth, that which gives occasion."

Christian liberty is not to live a lascivious life (characterized or expressing lust or lewdness; exciting lustful desires).

1 Peter 2:16–19
16 *As free, and not using your liberty for a cloke of maliciousness, but as the servants of God.*
17 *Honour all men. Love the brotherhood. Fear God. Honour the king.*
18 *Servants, be subject to your masters with all fear; not only to the good and gentle, but also to the forward.*
19 *For this is thankworthy, if a man for conscience toward God endure grief, suffering wrongfully.*

B. A Purpose (vv. 13c–15)

Through salvation, we are also given a holy purpose—to serve, love, and help one another.

1. To serve (13c)

Galatians 6:2
2 *Bear ye one another's burdens, and so fulfil the law of Christ.*

Christian liberty gives us the ability to have a spirit like this neighbor, to see the needs of those around us and meet those needs instead of worrying about fulfilling every ritual of the law.

2. To love (v. 14)

1 John 3:16–18
16 *Hereby perceive we the love of God, because he laid down his life for us: and we ought to lay down our lives for the brethren.*
17 *But whoso hath this world's good, and seeth his brother have need, and shutteth up his bowels of compassion from him, how dwelleth the love of God in him?*

> 18 My little children, let us not love in word, neither in tongue; but in deed and in truth.

Quote—You can give without loving, but you cannot love without giving.—Amy Carmichael

3. **To preserve (v. 15)**

   Paul explains in this verse that God's people are not to devour one another. Instead, we are to help each other survive in this race.

   ACTS 20:29

   > 29 For I know this, that after my departing shall grievous wolves enter in among you, not sparing the flock.

   Illustration—At times we probably feel it would be so much easier if we could be like Lucy in the old Peanuts cartoon: Lucy says to Charlie Brown, "I would have made a great evangelist." Charlie Brown answers, "Is that so?" She says, "Yes, I convinced that boy in front of me in school that my religion is better than his religion." Charlie Brown asked, "Well, how did you do that?" And Lucy answers, "I hit him over the head with my lunch box."

   1 CORINTHIANS 3:3

   > 3 For ye are yet carnal: for whereas there is among you envying, and strife, and divisions, are ye not carnal, and walk as men?

   Instead of allowing personality divisions, we are to love and serve one another.

Conclusion

Without a doubt, the Christian race is a difficult race to run. Its course is one through mountains and valleys. But if we keep our eyes focused on the finish line, we will finish our course where Christ waits to hand us our crowns and say, "Well done, my good and faithful servant."

OUTLINE SEVENTEEN

WALKING IN THE SPIRIT
GALATIANS 5:16–21

16 This I say then, Walk in the Spirit, and ye shall not fulfil the lust of the flesh.
17 For the flesh lusteth against the Spirit, and the Spirit against the flesh: and these are contrary the one to the other: so that ye cannot do the things that ye would.
18 But if ye be led of the Spirit, ye are not under the law.
19 Now the works of the flesh are manifest, which are these; Adultery, fornication, uncleanness, lasciviousness,
20 Idolatry, witchcraft, hatred, variance, emulations, wrath, strife, seditions, heresies,
21 Envyings, murders, drunkenness, revellings, and such like: of the which I tell you before, as I have also told you in time past, that they which do such things shall not inherit the kingdom of God.

Introduction

God did not create man to live in sin. He created us to abide in Him through His indwelling Spirit.

Ephesians 1:13

13 In whom ye also trusted after that ye heard the word of truth, the gospel of your salvation: in whom also after that ye believed, ye were sealed with that holy Spirit of promise.

We cannot bear fruit on our own.

John 15:1–4

1 I am the true vine, and my Father is the husbandman.
2 Every branch in me that beareth not fruit he taketh away: and every branch that beareth fruit, he purgeth it, that it may bring forth more fruit.
3 Now ye are clean through the word which I have spoken unto you.
4 Abide in me, and I in you. As the branch cannot bear fruit of itself, except it abide in the vine; no more can ye, except ye abide in me.

John 14:26

26 But the Comforter, which is the Holy Ghost, whom the Father will send in my name, he shall teach you all things, and bring all things to your remembrance, whatsoever I have said unto you.

We need to learn what it means to walk in the Spirit daily.

I. The Command to the Believer (v. 16)

A. *The Command to Walk*

When a person is saved, the inner man is cleansed by the blood, and he is indwelt by the Spirit.

The word *walk* means "to make one's way, progress; to make due use of opportunities; to regulate one's life; to conduct one's self—To walk is used to refer to the consistence." This word is in the imperative mood, giving a command. We are *commanded* to walk in the Spirit.

Walk also indicates a habitual practice. This would go along with Ephesians 5:18, to be filled with the Spirit. "To be filled" is yielding or submitting our will to allow the Holy Spirit to have control of our will and life.

To walk in the Spirit, then, would be living in a constant condition of maintaining a Spirit-filled life. Paul is telling these Galatians that the only way to be victorious Christians is to have a continual habit of living in the energizing power of the Holy Spirit.

B. The Consequence of Obedience

The word *fulfill* in Greek is *teleo* meaning, "to bring to a close, to finish, to end; to perform, execute, complete; to bring to completion or an end."

This word includes the negation ("not fulfill"). So if we walk habitually in the power of the Spirit, we will not fulfill the lusts of the flesh.

The word *lust* simply means "greatly desire."

Fruit does not grow naturally. Weeds grow naturally. The fruit of the Spirit grows supernaturally.

Quote—Other people don't create your spirit; they only reveal it.—Patrick Morley

II. The Competition within the Believer (vv. 17–21)

A. The Flesh Battles the Spirit (v. 17–18)

Along with many other passages in the New Testament, these two verses make it obvious that walking in the Spirit is not simply a matter of passive surrender. The Spirit-led life is a life of conflict because it is in constant combat with the old ways of the flesh that continue to tempt and seduce the believer.

ROMANS 7:18–19

18 For I know that in me (that is, in my flesh,) dwelleth no good thing: for to will is present with me; but how to perform that which is good I find not.

> 19 *For the good that I would I do not: but the evil which I would not, that I do.*

The flesh is that part of a believer that functions apart from and against the Spirit. It stands against the work of the Spirit in the believer's new heart. The unsaved person often regrets the sinful things he does because of guilt and/or painful consequences, but he does not have the spiritual warfare going on within him in the same way a believer has because he does not have the indwelling Spirit of God.

B. *The Flesh Brings Death (vv. 19–21)*

Better housing, transportation, education, jobs, income, medical care, and all other such things, desirable as they may be, can do nothing to solve man's basic problem which is the sin inside of him. No outward benefit can improve man inwardly. Instead, better outward conditions offer better and more sophisticated opportunities to do evil. Those very benefits themselves are often corrupted by the people they are designed to help.

Paul's list of the works of the flesh encompasses three general areas: immorality, religion, and human relationships.

1. **Through sexual immorality**
   - Adultery
   - Fornication: "permitting sexual thoughts and acts outside of marriage"
   - Uncleanness

   Illustration—The Roman world of Paul's day was corrupt. Corinth was known for its immorality and unclean living. In fact, *korinthiazethai* (to live like a Corinthian) meant to live an openly drunken and immoral lifestyle.

2. **Through religious idolatry**
   - Idolatry

- Witchcraft or sorcery

3. **Through human relationships**
    - Hatred
    - Variance: "quarrelsomeness"
    - Emulations: "to strive to imitate because of jealousy"
    - Wrath: "outbursts of anger"
    - Strife
    - Seditions: "having a spirit to stand apart; to create division"
    - Heresies
    - Envyings
    - Murders
    - Drunkenness
    - Revellings: "carousing in drunkenness"

According to verse 21B, the people who make a habitual practice of these things will not inherit the Kingdom of God because they are not saved.

Although many of these things are prevalent in our day, we must realize that Christians have been fighting against these lifestyles since the time of Paul and even before then. The promise God gives us is not that these kinds of people won't inherit the Earth, but that they won't inherit Heaven. We must keep in perspective that this war has been raging a long time, but we are on the winning side!

III. The Conquest for the Believer (v. 18)

A. *Yield to the Spirit (v. 18)*
Paul contrasts the Spirit and the law in this verse. He emphasizes that the Spirit produces fruit, but the law cannot produce righteousness.

Romans 8:12–13

12 *Therefore, brethren, we are debtors, not to the flesh, to live after the flesh.*

13 *For if ye live after the flesh, ye shall die: but if ye through the Spirit do mortify the deeds of the body, ye shall live.*

B. Don't Feed the Flesh

Romans 13:14

14 *But put ye on the Lord Jesus Christ, and make not provision for the flesh, to fulfil the lusts thereof.*

Matthew 6:13

13 *And lead us not into temptation, but deliver us from evil: For thine is the kingdom, and the power, and the glory, for ever. Amen.*

The most effective way for a Christian to oppose the desires and deeds of the flesh is to starve them to death, to "make no provision for the flesh" in regard to its lusts.

Conclusion

Walking in the Spirit is an essential part of the Christian life. In fact, the presence of the Holy Spirit is the most valuable asset that Christians have. We must allow the Holy Spirit to lead us in doing right and convict us when we do wrong.

Illustration—Many people go to the doctor for routine yearly check-ups. Some doctors practice what is known as "early detection." Their purpose is to find problems before they become too serious. They run series of tests to detect any potential problems and notify their patients of any areas of concern.

The Holy Spirit can act as our "early detection doctor." Periodically, we need to put ourselves under the check-up of the Spirit and allow Him to help us find areas of concern through "early detection."

OUTLINE EIGHTEEN

Walking with Love
Galatians 5:22–23

22 *But the fruit of the Spirit is love, joy, peace, longsuffering, gentleness, goodness, faith,*
23 *Meekness, temperance: against such there is no law.*

Introduction

The fruit of the Spirit is the fruit that comes from God Himself. It is this fruit that illustrates we are connected to the vine.

John 15:1, 5
1 *I am the true vine, and my Father is the husbandman.*
5 *I am the vine, ye are the branches: He that abideth in me, and I in him, the same bringeth forth much fruit: for without me ye can do nothing.*

The fruit of the Spirit is contrasted with the deeds of the flesh. Deeds of the flesh are done by a person's own efforts, whether he is saved or unsaved. However, the fruit of the Spirit is produced by God's own Spirit and only in the lives of those who belong to Him through faith in Jesus Christ.

There is a strong contrast between the deeds of the flesh and the fruit of the Spirit in that the products of the flesh are plural (*deeds* of the flesh), whereas the product of the Spirit is singular (*fruit* of the Spirit). The deeds of the flesh are varied and sullied. But the fruit of the Spirit—although multi-faceted—is the singular result of the Holy Spirit's work in our lives.

In this first outline on the fruit of the Spirit we begin with the first aspect of this fruit listed in Galatians 5—love.

1 John 3:16
16 *Hereby perceive we the love of God, because he laid down his life for us: and we ought to lay down our lives for the brethren.*

1 John 4:16
16 *And we have known and believed the love that God hath to us. God is love; and he that dwelleth in love dwelleth in God, and God in him.*

1 Peter 4:8
8 *And above all things have fervent charity among yourselves: for charity shall cover the multitude of sins.*

Young and old, rich and poor, believer and unbelievers all cry out for one singular thing—love.

Illustration—Madalyn Murray O'Hair, founder of American Atheists, vanished in 1995. When her diaries were found she often cried, "Somebody somewhere please love me."

I. The Meaning of Love

A. *Defined in Language*

The Greek word used for *love* here is *agape* which refers to a strong, sacrificial love.

Agape love is the deliberate effort, made with the help of God, to never seek anything but the best for others, even if they seek the worst for us.

Illustration—A mother gets up at 3:00 AM to help her sick child, not because she feels like it but because she has made a commitment. She has made a decision to love.

B. *Defined in Scripture*

1. **God is love.**
   1 JOHN 4:8
   8 He that loveth not knoweth not God; for God is love.

2. **God's love is everlasting.**
   JEREMIAH 31:3
   3 The LORD hath appeared of old unto me, saying, Yea, I have loved thee with an everlasting love: therefore with lovingkindness have I drawn thee.

   The word *everlasting* means "from vanishing point to vanishing point." God's love for us reaches from vanishing point to vanishing point.

   JOHN 13:1
   1 Now before the feast of the passover, when Jesus knew that his hour was come that he should depart out of this world unto the Father, having loved his own which were in the world, he loved them unto the end.

   Illustration—Emotional love wears off. A husband was coming out of anesthesia after a series of tests in the hospital. His wife was sitting at his bedside, when his eyes fluttered open and he muttered, "You are beautiful." Flattered, the wife continued the vigil. Later he woke up again and said, "You're cute!" "What happened to beautiful?" she asked. "The drugs are wearing off," the husband replied!

II. The Message of Love (1 Corinthians 13)

1 Corinthians 13:1–8

1 Though I speak with the tongues of men and of angels, and have not charity, I am become as sounding brass, or a tinkling cymbal.
2 And though I have the gift of prophecy, and understand all mysteries, and all knowledge; and though I have all faith, so that I could remove mountains, and have not charity, I am nothing.
3 And though I bestow all my goods to feed the poor, and though I give my body to be burned, and have not charity, it profiteth me nothing.
4 Charity suffereth long, and is kind; charity envieth not; charity vaunteth not itself, is not puffed up,
5 Doth not behave itself unseemly, seeketh not her own, is not easily provoked, thinketh no evil;
6 Rejoiceth not in iniquity, but rejoiceth in the truth;
7 Beareth all things, believeth all things, hopeth all things, endureth all things.
8 Charity never faileth: but whether there be prophecies, they shall fail; whether there be tongues, they shall cease; whether there be knowledge, it shall vanish away.

Quote—God knows that our relationships are more important than our accomplishments, and He challenges us to grow in His love.

A. The Helpfulness of Biblical Love (v. 4)

Here, Paul illustrates the nature of love.

1. Love is patient (slow to anger).

The word *patient* in Greek is *macro-thermos*, meaning, "a long time to boil."

Love practices being patient. The term "suffereth long" is a reference to having patience with people.

Quote—To dwell above with those we love, oh that will be glory, to dwell below with those we know, well, that's another story.—Author Unknown

Illustration—A woman said, "My husband is temperamental. He's 90 percent temper and 10 percent mental!"

Stephen in Acts 7 displayed godly, patient love to his persecutors.

ACTS 7:59–60
59 And they stoned Stephen, calling upon God, and saying, Lord Jesus, receive my spirit.
60 And he kneeled down, and cried with a loud voice, Lord, lay not this sin to their charge. And when he had said this, he fell asleep.

ROMANS 12:17
17 Recompense to no man evil for evil. Provide things honest in the sight of all men.

Illustration—President Lincoln had an early political rival named Edwin Stanton. Stanton called Lincoln "the original gorilla." When Lincoln was elected President, he chose Stanton to be his Secretary of War. Someone asked Lincoln why he chose Stanton, and he replied, "Because he's the best man for the job." At Lincoln's Funeral, Stanton said, "Here lies the greatest leader the world has ever known." Lincoln's non-retaliatory, patient spirit won out.

2. **Love is kind.**

Just as patience will *take* (endure) anything from others, kindness will *give* anything to others. To "be kind" means to be "useful, serving, and gracious."

1 PETER 3:8
8 Finally, be ye all of one mind, having compassion one of another, love as brethren, be pitiful, be courteous;

This aspect of love should characterize all of our relationships—starting in the home and extending to the church and to nonbelievers as well.

B. The Humility of Love (v. 4)

1. **Love is not jealous.**
   Love is not anxious against someone. Love and jealousy are mutually exclusive.

   We all face the temptation toward jealousy when someone else gets something a little better than what we have. If we act in the spirit of love, however, we will be glad for someone who is successful. We will not resent them.

   Jealousy is not a moderate sin. Just think of Cain!

   > **Proverbs 27:4**
   > 4 *Wrath is cruel, and anger is outrageous; but who is able to stand before envy?*

   The opposite of jealousy was the love of Jonathan for David (1 Samuel 20).

2. **Love does not brag.**
   Love does not talk conceitedly. It does not parade its accomplishments. Bragging is trying to make others jealous of what you have.

3. **Love is not arrogant.**
   Love is not puffed up.

   > **1 Corinthians 4:18–20**
   > 18 *Now some are puffed up, as though I would not come to you.*
   > 19 *But I will come to you shortly, if the Lord will, and will know, not the speech of them which are puffed up, but the power.*

   Quote—Arrogance is big-headed, but love is big-hearted.

   Illustration—Missionary William Carey (a missionary to India who knew twenty-three languages and dialects and translated Scripture into many of them) was at a dinner in England when he was asked, "I understand you once were a shoemaker?" Carey humbly replied, "Oh no, I was never a shoemaker, I was just a shoe repairman."

C. *The Holiness of Biblical Love (v. 5)*

1. **Love does not behave unseemly (unbecomingly, rudely).**
   The Corinthians were experts in unbecoming behavior.

   1 CORINTHIANS 11:21
   21 *For in eating every one taketh before other his own supper: and one is hungry, and another is drunken.*

   Love is gracious. Love does not behave itself gracelessly.

2. **Love does not seek its own.**
   PHILIPPIANS 2:4
   4 *Look not every man on his own things, but every man also on the things of others.*

3. **Love is not easily provoked (not easily aroused to anger).**
   1 PETER 2:23
   23 *Who, when he was reviled, reviled not again; when he suffered, he threatened not; but committed himself to him that judgeth righteously:*

4. **Love does not harbor evil.**
   Love does not "keep records" on evil. You are either a scorekeeper or a grace giver.

III. The Manifestation of Biblical Love

Quote—Christians should be God's love with skin on!

A. Our Love Is Displayed through Giving

1. **Give your time.**

   Illustration—One ingenious teenager, tired of reading bedtime stories to his little sister, decided to record several of her favorite stories on tape. He told her, "Now you can hear your stories anytime you want. Isn't that great?" She looked at the machine for a moment and then replied, "No. It hasn't got a lap."

2. **Give your communication.**

   1 PETER 3:8

   8 *Finally, be ye all of one mind, having compassion one of another, love as brethren, be pitiful, be courteous:*

3. **Give your forgiveness.**

   1 JOHN 4:20–21

   20 *If a man say, I love God, and hateth his brother, he is a liar: for he that loveth not his brother whom he hath seen, how can he love God whom he hath not seen?*

   21 *And this commandment have we from him, That he who loveth God love his brother also.*

B. God's Love Was Displayed through Giving

JOHN 3:16

16 *For God so loved the world, that he gave his only begotten Son, that whosoever believeth in him should not perish, but have everlasting life.*

Conclusion

Paul's exhortation on love to the Galatians and Corinthians extends to us today. Christ put such an emphasis on love as a motivator for action that He said the world will know we are His disciples if we have love for each other (John 13:25). May it be said of us, as individual believers and as churches, that we love each other and so love the world that we take them the gospel.

Outline Nineteen

Walking with Joy
Galatians 5:22–23

22 *But the fruit of the Spirit is love, joy, peace, longsuffering, gentleness, goodness, faith,*
23 *Meekness, temperance: against such there is no law.*

Introduction

Staying positive in a negative world is a difficult task. Throughout the Bible, however, Christians are commanded to have joy.

Nehemiah 8:10

10 *Then he said unto them, Go your way, eat the fat, and drink the sweet, and send portions unto them for whom nothing is prepared: for this day is holy unto our Lord: neither be ye sorry; for the joy of the Lord is your strength.*

Philippians 4:4

4 *Rejoice in the Lord alway: and again I say, Rejoice.*

In the New Testament we find the word *joy* about sixty times and the word *rejoice* about seventy-two times. The word *joy* is translated from the Greek word *chara*, meaning "a joy which foundation is found in God." Actually, the Greek words for *joy (chara)* and *grace (charis)* are almost identical. If we know God's grace, we can experience His joy because joy is produced by the Holy Spirit.

ROMANS 14:17

17 *For the kingdom of God is not meat and drink; but righteousness, and peace, and joy in the Holy Ghost.*

1 THESSALONIANS 1:6

6 *And ye became followers of us, and of the Lord, having received the word in much affliction, with joy of the Holy Ghost:*

We cannot know God's joy until we know God's love.

I. The Reasons for Our Joy

A. Joy Is the Result of Salvation

ROMANS 15:13

13 *Now the God of hope fill you with all joy and peace in believing, that ye may abound in hope, through the power of the Holy Ghost.*

1. We rejoice because of the love of God.

1 PETER 1:8

8 *Whom having not seen, ye love; in whom, though now ye see him not, yet believing, ye rejoice with joy unspeakable and full of glory:*

LUKE 2:10

10 *And the angel said unto them, Fear not: for, behold, I bring you good tidings of great joy, which shall be to all people.*

2. We rejoice because of the Book of Life.

Luke 10:20
20 *Notwithstanding in this rejoice not, that the spirits are subject unto you; but rather rejoice, because your names are written in heaven.*

B. Joy Is the Fruit of the Spirit

Galatians 5:22
22 *But the fruit of the Spirit is love, joy, peace, longsuffering, gentleness, goodness, faith,*

Romans 14:17
17 *For the kingdom of God is not meat and drink; but righteousness, and peace, and joy in the Holy Ghost.*

Joy is a disposition produced by the Holy Spirit.

II. The Resistance against Joy

In spite of the Holy Spirit's work in us, there are aspects of life that are continually resisting our joy in the Lord.

A. Bitterness

Hebrews 12:15
15 *Looking diligently lest any man fail of the grace of God; lest any root of bitterness springing up trouble you, and thereby many be defiled;*

B. *Suffering*

We can avoid bitterness by receiving God's grace to forgive, but we cannot avoid suffering. Suffering comes to all of us, and we have no control over it.

We do, however, have a choice in how we respond to suffering. When we abide in Christ through suffering, we find that suffering—this resister of joy—actually works to *further* our joy.

1 PETER 1:6–8

6 Wherein ye greatly rejoice, though now for a season, if need be, ye are in heaviness through manifold temptations:

7 That the trial of your faith, being much more precious than of gold that perisheth, though it be tried with fire, might be found unto praise and honour and glory at the appearing of Jesus Christ:

8 Whom having not seen, ye love; in whom, though now ye see him not, yet believing, ye rejoice with joy unspeakable and full of glory:

ROMANS 5:1–4

1 Therefore being justified by faith, we have peace with God through our Lord Jesus Christ:

2 By whom also we have access by faith into this grace wherein we stand, and rejoice in hope of the glory of God.

3 And not only so, but we glory in tribulations also: knowing that tribulation worketh patience;

4 And patience, experience; and experience, hope:

C. **Persecution**

MATTHEW 5:10–12

10 Blessed are they which are persecuted for righteousness' sake: for theirs is the kingdom of heaven.

11 Blessed are ye, when men shall revile you, and persecute you, and shall say all manner of evil against you falsely, for my sake.

12 Rejoice, and be exceeding glad: for great is your reward in heaven: for so persecuted they the prophets which were before you.

III. The Reinstatement of Our Joy

Joy is the byproduct of obedience.

PROVERBS 16:3

3 Commit thy works unto the LORD, and thy thoughts shall be established.

Here are four ways to develop joy:

A. *Through Our Singing*
The Bible says that we are to make a joyful noise unto the Lord.

JAMES 5:13
13 *Is any among you afflicted? let him pray. Is any merry? let him sing psalms.*

B. *Through Our Serving*
ACTS 20:24
24 *But none of these things move me, neither count I my life dear unto myself, so that I might finish my course with joy, and the ministry, which I have received of the Lord Jesus, to testify the gospel of the grace of God.*

C. *Through Our Soulwinning and Discipleship*
PROVERBS 11:30
30 *The fruit of the righteous is a tree of life; and he that winneth souls is wise.*

PHILIPPIANS 4:1
1 *Therefore, my brethren dearly beloved and longed for, my joy and crown, so stand fast in the Lord, my dearly beloved.*

D. *Through Our Stewardship*
Quote—A cold heart and a stingy hand go together.—John Charles Ryle

Quote—Laughter is an instant vacation. Giving is a two-week cruise—with pay.—Bob Hope

ACTS 20:35
35 *I have shewed you all things, how that so labouring ye ought to support the weak, and to remember the words of the Lord Jesus, how he said, It is more blessed to give than to receive.*

> **Quote**—The poorest man I know is the man who has nothing but money.—John D. Rockefeller, Jr.

2 Corinthians 8:2–3
2 How that in a great trial of affliction the abundance of their joy and their deep poverty abounded unto the riches of their liberality.
3 For to their power, I bear record, yea, and beyond their power they were willing of themselves;

Conclusion

Christian joy only comes through salvation. Those who have never experienced the unspeakable joy and peace that salvation brings will forever be searching for a substitute. But those who have experienced salvation, testify of its satisfaction.

Even believers, however, lose their joy. This does not mean they have lost their salvation, only the joy of it. Just as David did, we can ask that our joy be restored to us.

Psalm 51:12
12 Restore unto me the joy of thy salvation; and uphold me with thy free spirit.

It is God's desire that we be a joyful people. He wants to give us joy through His Spirit.

Hebrews 12:2
2 Looking unto Jesus the author and finisher of our faith; who for the joy that was set before him endured the cross, despising the shame, and is set down at the right hand of the throne of God.

OUTLINE TWENTY

Walking with Peace
Galatians 5:22–23

22 *But the fruit of the Spirit is love, joy, peace, longsuffering, gentleness, goodness, faith,*
23 *Meekness, temperance: against such there is no law.*

Introduction

The world is longing for peace—peace of mind, inner peace, and world peace. We hear about it every day.

Some seek peace in a bottle or pills. The more people seem to seek peace, the less they find.

The Old Testament word for peace is *shalom*. It means, "a desire or prayer that all is well with you." The New Testament word for peace means, "to bind together."

Peace is not merely the absence of war: it is the presence of Jesus. Peace is harmony and oneness with God's purposes.

I. Peace from Above

Jesus desires peace for each of us.

JOHN 14:27

27 *Peace I leave with you, my peace I give unto you: not as the world giveth, give I unto you. Let not your heart be troubled, neither let it be afraid.*

Christ's peace is a gift.

JOHN 16:33

33 *These things I have spoken unto you, that in me ye might have peace. In the world ye shall have tribulation: but be of good cheer; I have overcome the world.*

A. **Peace with God Is Available**

ROMANS 5:1

1 *Therefore being justified by faith, we have peace with God through our Lord Jesus Christ:*

B. **Peace Is Available through Jesus Christ**

1. **Sin separated men from God.**

   Sin created hostility between man and God. That sin created a conflict.

   ROMANS 5:12

   12 *Wherefore, as by one man sin entered into the world, and death by sin; and so death passed upon all men, for that all have sinned:*

2. **Jesus came to make peace.**

   COLOSSIANS 1:20

   20 *And, having made peace through the blood of his cross, by him to reconcile all things unto himself; by him, I say, whether they be things in earth, or things in heaven.*

Guilt is the number one destroyer of peace. Yet Jesus died to remove guilt. Religion puts guilt back on its followers, telling them that in order for them to be guilt-free, they must follow a set of rules, sacraments, and rituals. Christ made us free from the guilt of sin when He conquered death and sin. He gives us the gift of peace through His sacrifice.

II. Peace for Within

Illustration—There once was a Peanuts cartoon with Lucy saying to Charlie Brown, "I hate everything. I hate everybody. I hate the whole wide world!" Charlie says, "But I thought you had inner peace." Lucy replies, "I do have inner peace. But I still have outer obnoxiousness."

A. *Peace Is a Grace of the Holy Spirit*

Peace is a disposition created by the Holy Spirit, and only the Holy Spirit can spread this God-given peace into every believer's heart.

ROMANS 15:13
13 *Now the God of hope fill you with all joy and peace in believing, that ye may abound in hope, through the power of the Holy Ghost.*

B. *God's Peace Is beyond Description*

PHILIPPIANS 4:6–7
6 *Be careful for nothing; but in every thing by prayer and supplication with thanksgiving let your requests be made known unto God.*
7 *And the peace of God, which passeth all understanding, shall keep your hearts and minds through Christ Jesus.*

Illustration—The word *worry* is derived from the German word *wergen* which means "to choke."

Illustration—A group of Korean Christians were being persecuted for their faith. When asked how they remained so faithful even during persecution, they answered, "We are just like nails. The harder you drive us, the deeper you drive us. The deeper you drive us, the more peaceful it becomes."

God's peace is an invincible force in the heart of a Christian enduring trial.

1. **God's peace is sustained by the Word of God.**
   ISAIAH 26:3
   > 3 Thou wilt keep him in perfect peace, whose mind is stayed on thee: because he trusteth in thee.

   PSALM 119:165
   > 165 Great peace have they which love thy law: and nothing shall offend them.

2. **God's peace will rule your heart.**
   Quote—Confidence is the courage to be at ease. —Daniel Maher

   COLOSSIANS 3:15
   > 15 And let the peace of God rule in your hearts, to the which also ye are called in one body; and be ye thankful.

   Ultimately, God's peace will enable you to have peace with others.

III. Peace All Around

HEBREWS 12:14
> 14 Follow peace with all men, and holiness, without which no man shall see the Lord:

Most of our problems in life are people problems. Yet peace in the heart of the Christian should spread to every relationship of our lives.

Romans 12:18
18 *If it be possible, as much as lieth in you, live peaceably with all men.*

A. *In Our Homes*
Illustration—A husband says to his wife as he turns on the first football game of the year: "Is there anything you want to say before the season starts?"

Colossians 3:15
15 *And let the peace of God rule in your hearts, to the which also ye are called in one body; and be ye thankful.*

Illustration—A woman returned home from a holiday shopping spree with her arms loaded with packages. Her husband met her at the door and said, "What did you buy? With prices as high as they are, I'll bet you spent a fortune. I hate to think what has happened to our nest egg." "I'll tell you what happened to our nest egg," his wife said defensively as she began to put her packages on the dining room table. "The old hen got tired of sitting on it."

B. *In Our Church*
1 Corinthians 14:33
33 *For God is not the author of confusion, but of peace, as in all churches of the saints.*

Romans 16:17
17 *Now I beseech you, brethren, mark them which cause divisions and offences contrary to the doctrine which ye have learned; and avoid them.*

Ephesians 4:3
3 *Endeavouring to keep the unity of the Spirit in the bond of peace.*

C. In Our World

1. By preaching Christ

ROMANS 3:17–18

17 *And the way of peace have they not known:*
18 *There is no fear of God before their eyes.*

EPHESIANS 6:15

15 *And your feet shod with the preparation of the gospel of peace;*

2. By praying for our leaders

1 TIMOTHY 2:1–4

1 *I exhort therefore, that, first of all, supplications, prayers, intercessions, and giving of thanks, be made for all men;*
2 *For kings, and for all that are in authority; that we may lead a quiet and peaceable life in all godliness and honesty.*
3 *For this is good and acceptable in the sight of God our Saviour;*
4 *Who will have all men to be saved, and to come unto the knowledge of the truth.*

3. By expecting the return of our Lord

The world leaders are hoping to bring peace, but throughout history they have failed miserably. The Bible promises that political leaders will promise peace but will never bring it. Only Christ can offer true, everlasting peace.

1 THESSALONIANS 5:1–4

1 *But of the times and the seasons, brethren, ye have no need that I write unto you.*
2 *For yourselves know perfectly that the day of the Lord so cometh as a thief in the night.*

3 *For when they shall say, Peace and safety; then sudden destruction cometh upon them, as travail upon a woman with child; and they shall not escape.*
4 *But ye, brethren, are not in darkness, that that day should overtake you as a thief.*

Isaiah 9:6

6 *For unto us a child is born, unto us a son is given: and the government shall be upon his shoulder: and his name shall be called Wonderful, Counsellor, The mighty God, The everlasting Father, The Prince of Peace.*

Conclusion

When we walk in the Spirit, we will have peace from above, within, and all around. When unbelievers see the peace and joy that believers possess, they will desire to know our source of joy, the Lord Jesus Christ.

Outline Twenty-One

Walking with Longsuffering
Galatians 5:22–23

22 *But the fruit of the Spirit is love, joy, peace, longsuffering, gentleness, goodness, faith,*
23 *Meekness, temperance: against such there is no law.*

Introduction

Illustration—The area of Indio, California, is known for its date trees. Each year, the city holds an annual date festival where they sell their famous date shakes. The date palms produce about one hundred pounds of fruit annually. One quality of date trees is that they live extraordinarily long lives. In fact, they don't even bear fruit for the first four years, and their most productive years of fruit bearing begins around age eighty. Their productivity is a testimony to their patience.

In this passage, Paul mentions the fruit of the Spirit, longsuffering. The Greek word for *longsuffering* is made up of two words: *makro*, meaning "slow" and *thumos*, meaning "wrath." Thus, it means "slow to wrath."

Thankfully, patience is an attribute of God.

Exodus 34:6
6 And the L ORD passed by before him, and proclaimed, The L ORD, The L ORD God, merciful and gracious, longsuffering, and abundant in goodness and truth,

It is also an attribute He commands in His children.

Ephesians 4:26
26 Be ye angry, and sin not: let not the sun go down upon your wrath:

We live in a day of quick retribution. Not enough people practice the patience of the Bible because most people are not born with a lot of patience.

Illustration—We all should be a little more like the boy standing at the end of the escalator. The sales lady asked, "Son are you lost?" "No ma'am, I'm waiting for my chewing gum to come back."

The fruit of longsuffering is not developed with a spirit of self-determination. It is developed by the Holy Spirit.

So, what does longsuffering do?

I. The Perseverance of Longsuffering

Longsuffering enables us to persevere on a difficult day.

2 Corinthians 6:4
4 But in all things approving ourselves as the ministers of God, in much patience, in afflictions, in necessities, in distresses,

James 5:10
10 Take, my brethren, the prophets, who have spoken in the name of the Lord, for an example of suffering affliction, and of patience.

A. *We Persevere because of God's Purpose*

1. **To correct us**
   HEBREWS 12:6–7
   6   *For whom the Lord loveth he chasteneth, and scourgeth every son whom he receiveth.*
   7   *If ye endure chastening, God dealeth with you as with sons; for what son is he whom the father chasteneth not?*

2. **To challenge us**
   PSALM 119:71
   71   *It is good for me that I have been afflicted; that I might learn thy statutes.*

3. **To use us**
   GENESIS 50:20
   20   *But as for you, ye thought evil against me; but God meant it unto good, to bring to pass, as it is this day, to save much people alive.*

   Illustration—When Joseph was sold into slavery by his brothers, he had no idea how God would one day use him. Joseph's longsuffering through trials and testing allowed him to be used by God in a great way.

B. ***We Persevere because of God's Priority***
    God's priority is to conform us into the image of His Son.

   ROMANS 8:28–29
   28   *And we know that all things work together for good to them that love God, to them who are the called according to his purpose.*
   29   *For whom he did foreknow, he also did predestinate to be conformed to the image of his Son, that he might be the firstborn among many brethren.*

   Quote—In adversity, we want God to do a removing job when He wants to do an improving job.

Our willingness to wait on the Lord is an expression of our faith.

II. The Influence of Longsuffering

Quote—Longsuffering is the grace of the man who could revenge himself and does not.—Chrysostom

When we exercise longsuffering, we will have godly influence with people in our lives.

A. *With Our Family*

Illustration—Someone once wrote, "Who can ever forget Winston Churchill's immortal words: 'We shall fight on the beaches, we shall fight on the landing grounds, we shall fight in the fields and in the streets, we shall fight in the hills.' It sounds exactly like our family vacation."

Sometimes we seem to have the least amount of patience with those closest to us. Instead of acting, we react. However, the Holy Spirit can enable us to be patient with our family.

Quote—A good marriage is not the result of finding the right person: it is a result of being the right person.

Ephesians 4:29
> 29 *Let no corrupt communication proceed out of your mouth, but that which is good to the use of edifying, that it may minister grace unto the hearers.*

We need wisdom and longsuffering to see problems from our spouses' point of view.

B. *With Others around Us*

Like most fruits of the Spirit, patience is the product of love.

1 Corinthians 13:4

4 *Charity suffereth long, and is kind; charity envieth not; charity vaunteth not itself, is not puffed up,*

Charity suffers with the weaknesses, ignorance, and error of others. It waits for God to accomplish His divine purposes.

Romans 12:19

19 *Dearly beloved, avenge not yourselves, but rather give place unto wrath: for it is written, Vengeance is mine; I will repay, saith the Lord.*

1. Neighbors
2. Coworkers
3. Friends

Ephesians 4:1–3

1 *I therefore, the prisoner of the Lord, beseech you that ye walk worthy of the vocation wherewith ye are called,*
2 *With all lowliness and meekness, with longsuffering, forbearing one another in love;*
3 *Endeavouring to keep the unity of the Spirit in the bond of peace.*

1 Peter 2:23

23 *Who, when he was reviled, reviled not again; when he suffered, he threatened not; but committed himself to him that judgeth righteously:*

III. The Deliverance of Longsuffering

A. *The Deliverance of Salvation*

2 Peter 3:9

9 *The Lord is not slack concerning his promise, as some men count slackness; but is longsuffering to us-ward, not willing that any should perish, but that all should come to repentance.*

God's desire is for every lost person to repent and receive Christ. Because of His longsuffering, we have been saved and so can others.

1 Timothy 1:16
16 *Howbeit for this cause I obtained mercy, that in me first Jesus Christ might shew forth all longsuffering, for a pattern to them which should hereafter believe on him to life everlasting.*

B. ***The Deliverance of the Second Coming***
James 5:8
8 *Be ye also patient; stablish your hearts: for the coming of the Lord draweth nigh.*

Illustration—I once read of parents who decided to let their three-year-old son record the message for their home answering machine. The rehearsals went smoothly: "Mommy and Daddy can't come to the phone right now. If you'll leave your name, phone number, and a brief message, they'll get back to you as soon as possible." Then came the test. They pressed the record button and their son said sweetly, "Mommy and Daddy can't come to the phone right now. If you'll leave your name, phone number, and a brief message, they'll get back to you as soon as Jesus comes."

2 Peter 3:13–15
13 *Nevertheless we, according to his promise, look for new heavens and a new earth, wherein dwelleth righteousness.*
14 *Wherefore, beloved, seeing that ye look for such things, be diligent that ye may be found of him in peace, without spot, and blameless.*
15 *And account that the longsuffering of our Lord is salvation; even as our beloved brother Paul also according to the wisdom given unto him hath written unto you;*

Conclusion

We all face challenges on a daily basis, but the Holy Spirit has power to impart patience for every situation. Through the longsuffering the Holy Spirit gives, we can persevere, allowing us to grow in God's purpose. We can have godly influence on our family and friends. And we can have deliverance through salvation and Christ's return.

OUTLINE TWENTY-TWO

WALKING WITH GENTLENESS
GALATIANS 5:22–23

22 *But the fruit of the Spirit is love, joy, peace, longsuffering, gentleness, goodness, faith,*

23 *Meekness, temperance: against such there is no law.*

Introduction

Webster defines *gentleness* as "noble, chivalrous: as a gentle knight; generous, kind."

Quote—I will speak ill of no man, not even in the matter of truth, but rather excuse the faults I hear, and, upon proper occasions, speak all the good I know of everybody.—Benjamin Franklin

Gentleness or kindness is the fruit that will make or break our Christian testimony. In society as a whole, gentleness is hard to come by. In the church, however, gentleness should be something that is frequently named among us.

I. An Illustration of Gentleness

The Lord Himself is the personification of gentleness.

Psalm 117:1–2

1   *O praise the Lord, all ye nations: praise him, all ye people.*
2   *For his merciful kindness is great toward us: and the truth of the Lord endureth for ever. Praise ye the Lord.*

A. The Character of Jesus

Jesus did not have to die, yet He voluntarily went to the cross.

1 Peter 2:21–24

21 *For even hereunto were ye called: because Christ also suffered for us, leaving us an example, that ye should follow his steps:*
22 *Who did no sin, neither was guile found in his mouth:*
23 *Who, when he was reviled, reviled not again; when he suffered, he threatened not; but committed himself to him that judgeth righteously:*
24 *Who his own self bare our sins in his own body on the tree, that we, being dead to sins, should live unto righteousness: by whose stripes ye were healed.*

B. The Compassion of Jesus

1. **In His kindness, He offers salvation.**

   Titus 3:4–7

   4   *But after that the kindness and love of God our Saviour toward man appeared,*
   5   *Not by works of righteousness which we have done, but according to his mercy he saved us, by the washing of regeneration, and renewing of the Holy Ghost;*
   6   *Which he shed on us abundantly through Jesus Christ our Saviour;*
   7   *That being justified by his grace, we should be made heirs according to the hope of eternal life.*

EPHESIANS 2:7–9

7 *That in the ages to come he might shew the exceeding riches of his grace in his kindness toward us through Christ Jesus.*

8 *For by grace are ye saved through faith; and that not of yourselves: it is the gift of God:*

9 *Not of works, lest any man should boast.*

2. **His kindness leads us to repentance.**

ROMANS 2:4

4 *Or despisest thou the riches of his goodness and forbearance and longsuffering; not knowing that the goodness of God leadeth thee to repentance?*

II. An Infusion of Gentleness

We are, of course, grateful for the gentleness of God. But the Holy Spirit wants to infuse this gentleness into our lives as well.

A. *Through Sensitivity*

No matter how many Scriptures we have memorized or how many convictions we have, if we do not have kindness, none of these things matter. As Christians, we must be sensitive to the needs of others.

PHILIPPIANS 2:4–5

4 *Look not every man on his own things, but every man also on the things of others.*

5 *Let this mind be in you, which was also in Christ Jesus:*

Illustration—A man once said to his colleague, "Few things upset my wife. It makes me feel rather special to be one of them."

B. *Through Sympathy*

ROMANS 12:15

15 *Rejoice with them that do rejoice, and weep with them that weep.*

2 Timothy 2:24–26

24 And the servant of the Lord must not strive; but be gentle unto all men, apt to teach, patient,

25 In meekness instructing those that oppose themselves; if God peradventure will give them repentance to the acknowledging of the truth;

26 And that they may recover themselves out of the snare of the devil, who are taken captive by him at his will.

C. Through Spontaneity
Galatians 6:10

10 As we have therefore opportunity, let us do good unto all men, especially unto them who are of the household of faith.

III. An Inducement to Gentleness

A. We Are Empowered by the Spirit
Ephesians 5:18

18 And be not drunk with wine, wherein is excess; but be filled with the Spirit;

1. **In our homes**
   Illustration—A little five-year-old boy one day was playing with his two-year-old brother when the two-year-old reached up and yanked his older brother's hair. He screamed in pain, and his mother came rushing in. He cried and said that his younger brother had pulled his hair. His mom said, "Well, he's only two years old, and he doesn't know what it's like to have his hair pulled." The mom left, but seconds later she heard a scream from the bedroom. This time it was the two year old screaming in pain. She rushed in and asked what had happened, to which the five year old explained, "You said he didn't know what it felt like. Well, now he does."

2. **In our community**
   An unkind spirit in our church toward our community and community leaders will turn people away from the message of Christ.

   COLOSSIANS 3:12–13
   12 Put on therefore, as the elect of God, holy and beloved, bowels of mercies, kindness, humbleness of mind, meekness, longsuffering;
   13 Forbearing one another, and forgiving one another, if any man have a quarrel against any: even as Christ forgave you, so also do ye.

   - To those in need

   Illustration—Jesus helped the man at Bethesda and the woman at the well. Both people were in great need.

   - To those who oppose us

3. **In our church**
   Illustration—An usher speaking to another usher said, "We have nothing but good, kind Christians in this church—until you try to seat someone else in their pew."

B. *We Are Encouraged by the Testimony of Jesus*
When we think of how Jesus forgave us, we are encouraged and empowered to show kindness to others around us.

EPHESIANS 4:30–32
30 And grieve not the holy Spirit of God, whereby ye are sealed unto the day of redemption.
31 Let all bitterness, and wrath, and anger, and clamour, and evil speaking, be put away from you, with all malice:
32 And be ye kind one to another, tenderhearted, forgiving one another, even as God for Christ's sake hath forgiven you.

Conclusion

In a society where gentleness and kindness are lacking, we as Christians must display the gentleness of Christ to each other, our families, and our community. However, gentleness will not come to us through perseverance or determination. It will only come as we walk in the Spirit and produce His fruit.

OUTLINE TWENTY-THREE

WALKING WITH GOODNESS
GALATIANS 5:22–23

22 *But the fruit of the Spirit is love, joy, peace, longsuffering, gentleness, goodness, faith,*
23 *Meekness, temperance: against such there is no law.*

Introduction

EPHESIANS 5:8–10

8 *For ye were sometimes darkness, but now are ye light in the Lord: walk as children of light:*
9 *For the fruit of the Spirit is in all goodness and righteousness and truth;*
10 *Proving what is acceptable unto the Lord.*

Goodness is defined as "uprightness of heart and life; virtue equipped and ready at every point."

Illustration—When a family was going on an extended vacation, they asked their nine-year-old neighbor, Mike, about taking care of the family dog. They explained that the job would require feeding, watering, grooming, walking, and spending plenty of time playing with the dog and giving her lots of love. After covering the job description, they asked what the job would be worth to him. The little boy replied, "I'll give you ten bucks."

GALATIANS 6:10
10 *As we have therefore opportunity, let us do good unto all men, especially unto them who are of the household of faith.*

There are various ways people interpret the word *good*:

- To some, goodness revolves around anything that increases their pleasure. However, we know that even non-pleasurable seasons can be good for us.

- Some say knowledge brings goodness. They say if we can increase knowledge of good, there will be no evil. But knowing what is good has never guaranteed that we would do it.

- Some equate goodness with not doing certain things. "I didn't eat chocolate—I was good!" Or "I did not curse, so I am good."

- Jesus displayed the goodness of God.

ACTS 10:38
38 *How God anointed Jesus of Nazareth with the Holy Ghost and with power: who went about doing good, and healing all that were oppressed of the devil; for God was with him.*

Goodness is supernatural. It is not something we can produce on our own; it must be the fruit of the Holy Spirit within us. How does it develop in our lives?

I. Realize Our Inability to Produce God's Goodness

A. Because of Our Human Nature
There are those who say man is inherently good, but there are two reasons I do not believe this: First, I believe the Bible. Second, I am a parent!

Scripture paints a very different picture of our nature than we like to portray.

Romans 5:12

12 *Wherefore, as by one man sin entered into the world, and death by sin; and so death passed upon all men, for that all have sinned:*

Illustration—I once heard a secular humanist say that his belief was in the complete, inherent goodness of man. I wondered what planet he had been living on lately.

Romans 3:12

12 *They are all gone out of the way, they are together become unprofitable; there is none that doeth good, no, not one.*

B. Because of the Flesh

Even a Christian, in the flesh, can do terrible things.

Romans 7:18

18 *For I know that in me (that is, in my flesh,) dwelleth no good thing: for to will is present with me; but how to perform that which is good I find not.*

II. Rely on the Holy Spirit for Goodness

A. We Are Born of the Spirit

The new birth is a spiritual process.

John 3:5–7

5 *Jesus answered, Verily, verily, I say unto thee, Except a man be born of water and of the Spirit, he cannot enter into the kingdom of God.*

6 *That which is born of the flesh is flesh; and that which is born of the Spirit is spirit.*

7 *Marvel not that I said unto thee, Ye must be born again.*

Goodness can only come about by the Holy Spirit through a spiritual process.

Acts 11:24
24 *For he was a good man, and full of the Holy Ghost and of faith: and much people was added unto the Lord.*

B. We Receive a Divine Nature
2 Peter 1:3–4
3 *According as his divine power hath given unto us all things that pertain unto life and godliness, through the knowledge of him that hath called us to glory and virtue:*
4 *Whereby are given unto us exceeding great and precious promises: that by these ye might be partakers of the divine nature, having escaped the corruption that is in the world through lust.*

2 Corinthians 5:17
17 *Therefore if any man be in Christ, he is a new creature: old things are passed away; behold, all things are become new.*

C. We Must Walk in the Spirit
Galatians 5:16
16 *This I say then, Walk in the Spirit, and ye shall not fulfil the lust of the flesh.*

III. Reveal the Goodness of God to a Lost World.

Being good is what we are on the inside. *Doing* good is what people see on the outside. Good living is the fruit of the Spirit.

There are three ways we can reveal goodness:

A. Goodness Is Found in the Word of God
We don't know what is good by our own feelings.

Micah 6:8
> 8 He hath shewed thee, O man, what is good; and what doth the Lord require of thee, but to do justly, and to love mercy, and to walk humbly with thy God?

We cannot be a "good" husband or wife, apart from the Word of God.

B. *Goodness Is Cultivated through Godly Fellowship*
Hebrews 10:24
> 24 And let us consider one another to provoke unto love and to good works:

Quote—Do all the good you can, by all the means you can, in all the ways you can, in all the places you can, at all the times you can, to all the people you can and as long as you can.—John Wesley

C. *Goodness Is Revealed through a Walk with Christ*
Ephesians 2:8–10
> 8 For by grace are ye saved through faith; and that not of yourselves: it is the gift of God:
> 9 Not of works, lest any man should boast.
> 10 For we are his workmanship, created in Christ Jesus unto good works, which God hath before ordained that we should walk in them.

We should not brag about fruit because it is all to the glory of God.

1. The good work of witnessing
Matthew 5:16
> 16 Let your light so shine before men, that they may see your good works, and glorify your Father which is in heaven.

2. **The good work of serving**
   - At home

   ROMANS 12:21

   21 Be not overcome of evil, but overcome evil with good.

   - At church

   ACTS 9:39

   39 Then Peter arose and went with them. When he was come, they brought him into the upper chamber: and all the widows stood by him weeping, and shewing the coats and garments which Dorcas made, while she was with them.

Conclusion

If we as Christians are going to influence our churches, communities, and our own families, we must first realize our inability to produce God's goodness on our own. We must then rely on the Holy Spirit to produce goodness through us and reveal the goodness of God to a lost world.

OUTLINE TWENTY-FOUR

WALKING WITH FAITH
GALATIANS 5:22–23

22 *But the fruit of the Spirit is love, joy, peace, longsuffering, gentleness, goodness, faith,*
23 *Meekness, temperance: against such there is no law.*

Introduction

The word *faith* is used three different ways in the book of Galatians.

- Galatians 1:23 refers to "the faith," in context of the Christian gospel.
- Galatians 3:14 refers to faith for salvation.
- Galatians 5:22 refers to faithfulness in fulfilling our Christian duties.

In a sense, our faith should produce faithfulness. Faithfulness is the Christian character produced by the Holy Spirit, enabling us to be reliable or dependable.

There seems to be a short supply of faithfulness today. A lack of faithfulness is seen in the corporate world, the family realm, and sometimes in the church. The Holy Spirit, however, can make us trustworthy or reliable.

Faithfulness is doing our duty until our duty is done. Every great servant of God has been a faithful servant, including the Lord Jesus Christ.

HEBREWS 3:1–2
1   Wherefore, holy brethren, partakers of the heavenly calling, consider the Apostle and High Priest of our profession, Christ Jesus;
2   Who was faithful to him that appointed him, as also Moses was faithful in all his house.

We need the kind of faithfulness the Holy Spirit can produce. The disciples of Christ found the Holy Spirit made the difference for them in the area of faithfulness. Previously, when the Lord had needed them the most, they were faithless. Then came the day of Pentecost and the filling of the Holy Spirit. These same men were faithful witnesses and ultimately died a faithful martyr's death.

Illustration—Many of the early missionaries exhibited great faithfulness. William Carey, the great missionary to India saw few early results to his labor. He wrote to a friend, "Pray for us that we may be faithful to the end."

I. The Faithfulness of God

A. *Faithful in His Attributes*
HEBREWS 10:23
23 Let us hold fast the profession of our faith without wavering; (for he is faithful that promised;)

HEBREWS 11:11
11 Through faith also Sara herself received strength to conceive seed, and was delivered of a child when she was past age, because she judged him faithful who had promised.

DEUTERONOMY 7:9
9   Know therefore that the LORD thy God, he is God, the faithful God, which keepeth covenant and mercy with

> them that love him and keep his commandments to a thousand generations;

Even when we are faithless, God is faithful.

2 Timothy 2:13
> 13 If we believe not, yet he abideth faithful: he cannot deny himself.

1. **He is faithful during temptation.**
   1 Corinthians 10:13
   > 13 There hath no temptation taken you but such as is common to man: but God is faithful, who will not suffer you to be tempted above that ye are able; but will with the temptation also make a way to escape, that ye may be able to bear it.

2. **He is faithful during trials.**
   Illustration—A mother and her little four-year-old daughter were preparing to retire for the night. The child was afraid of the dark, and the mother, on this occasion alone with the child, felt fearful also. When the light was out, the child caught a glimpse of the moon outside the window. "Mother," she asked, "is the moon God's light?" "Yes," said the mother. The next question was, "Will God put out His light and go to sleep?" The mother replied, "No, my child, God never goes to sleep." Then out of the simplicity of a child's faith, she said that which gave reassurance to the fearful mother, "Well, as long as God is awake, there is no sense both of us staying awake." (sermoncentral.com)

B. *Faithful in His Word*
   Psalm 119:86
   > 86 All thy commandments are faithful: they persecute me wrongfully; help thou me.

Psalm 119:89

89 For ever, O Lord, thy word is settled in heaven.

II. The Fervency of God's People

Illustration—Two frogs fell into a tub of cream. The one looked at the high sides of the tub which were too difficult to crawl over and said, "It is hopeless." So he resigned himself to death, relaxed, and sank to the bottom. The other one determined to keep swimming as long as he could. "Something might happen," he said. And it did. He kept kicking and churning, and finally he found himself on a solid platform of butter and jumped to safety. Sometimes faithfulness and patience make the difference!

A. *God Requires Faithfulness*

God does not require talent. He only requires our faithfulness.

1 Corinthians 4:2

2 Moreover it is required in stewards, that a man be found faithful.

1. Faithful in our work places

Colossians 3:23

23 And whatsoever ye do, do it heartily, as to the Lord, and not unto men;

2. Faithful to our families

Ephesians 5:25–26

25 Husbands, love your wives, even as Christ also loved the church, and gave himself for it;

26 That he might sanctify and cleanse it with the washing of water by the word,

3. Faithful in our stewardship

Luke 16:10–12

10 He that is faithful in that which is least is faithful also in much: and he that is unjust in the least is unjust also in much.

> *11 If therefore ye have not been faithful in the unrighteous mammon, who will commit to your trust the true riches?*
>
> *12 And if ye have not been faithful in that which is another man's, who shall give you that which is your own?*

As we are faithful with this world's goods, we will be faithful in spiritual matters as well.

4. Faithful in our church attendance
HEBREWS 10:25

> *25 Not forsaking the assembling of ourselves together, as the manner of some is; but exhorting one another: and so much the more, as ye see the day approaching.*

Quote—I don't know why some people change churches—what difference does it make which one you stay home from?

B. God Produces Faithfulness

The Holy Spirit is in our lives to make our character more like Jesus. Faithfulness is the disposition of the Holy Spirit.

III. Our Examination of Faithfulness

One day we will be examined for our faithfulness.

1 CORINTHIANS 4:2–5

> *2 Moreover it is required in stewards, that a man be found faithful.*
>
> *3 But with me it is a very small thing that I should be judged of you, or of man's judgment: yea, I judge not mine own self.*
>
> *4 For I know nothing by myself; yet am I not hereby justified: but he that judgeth me is the Lord.*
>
> *5 Therefore judge nothing before the time, until the Lord come, who both will bring to light the hidden things of darkness, and will make manifest the counsels of the hearts: and then shall every man have praise of God.*

A. We All Have Different Opportunities
MATTHEW 25:14–21

14 For the kingdom of heaven is as a man travelling into a far country, who called his own servants, and delivered unto them his goods.

15 And unto one he gave five talents, to another two, and to another one; to every man according to his several ability; and straightway took his journey.

16 Then he that had received the five talents went and traded with the same, and made them other five talents.

17 And likewise he that had received two, he also gained other two.

18 But he that had received one went and digged in the earth, and hid his lord's money.

19 After a long time the lord of those servants cometh, and reckoneth with them.

20 And so he that had received five talents came and brought other five talents, saying, Lord, thou deliveredst unto me five talents: behold, I have gained beside them five talents more.

21 His lord said unto him, Well done, thou good and faithful servant: thou hast been faithful over a few things, I will make thee ruler over many things: enter thou into the joy of thy lord.

The talents in this parable showed that unequal gifts, if used with equal faithfulness, will be equally rewarded.

B. We Will All Be Examined According to Our Faithfulness
MATTHEW 25:19

19 After a long time the lord of those servants cometh, and reckoneth with them.

We are not called to be successful: we are called to be faithful.

Revelation 2:10

10 *Fear none of those things which thou shalt suffer: behold, the devil shall cast some of you into prison, that ye may be tried; and ye shall have tribulation ten days: be thou faithful unto death, and I will give thee a crown of life.*

Conclusion

Faithfulness is not always easy, but Christ commands us to walk in faithfulness by His Spirit. Perhaps, if we keep in our minds the ultimate goal of pleasing our Lord and Saviour, we will find it a little easier to remain faithful in these difficult times.

Matthew 25:21

21 *His lord said unto him, Well done, thou good and faithful servant: thou hast been faithful over a few things, I will make thee ruler over many things: enter thou into the joy of thy lord.*

OUTLINE TWENTY-FIVE

WALKING WITH MEEKNESS
GALATIANS 5:22–23

22 *But the fruit of the Spirit is love, joy, peace, longsuffering, gentleness, goodness, faith,*
23 *Meekness, temperance: against such there is no law.*

Introduction

Meekness is a word that we rarely hear in society today. The media does not highlight stories of meekness. There is not "Top Ten Meekest People of the Year" award given by any magazine. Perhaps this is because meekness is often associated with a lack of personality or strength. Meekness, however, is not weakness. In fact, quite the opposite is true because uncommon strength is needed to be meek.

The definition of meekness is "a submissive and teachable spirit toward God that reveals itself in genuine consideration toward others." Meekness is willingness to yield, but it is never spineless. Meekness requires that we stoop down to meet the emotional needs of others.

Quote—God uses broken things. It takes broken soil to produce a crop, broken clouds to give rain, broken grain to give bread, broken bread to give strength. It is the broken alabaster box that gives forth perfume. It is Peter, weeping bitterly, who returns to greater power than ever.
—Vance Havner

Jesus Himself was meek.

MATTHEW 21:5
5   Tell ye the daughter of Sion, Behold, thy King cometh unto thee, meek, and sitting upon an ass, and a colt the foal of an ass.

I. The Origin of Meekness

A. Meekness Is Produced by the Holy Spirit

1. The meek will learn of God.

PSALM 25:9
9   The meek will he guide in judgment: and the meek will he teach his way.

In this self-willed day, meekness is something that must be imparted by the Holy Spirit.

Illustration—Two wives were doing their laundry at a laundromat. They were both mending their husbands' pants. One wife said, "My husband is so miserable. Nothing goes right at work, and he can't find anything good on television. Our home is a place of despair. When we go to church, the song leader is terrible and the Pastor is an idiot." The other wife said "My husband is so excited. He can't wait to go to church. He loves the sermons. We laugh all the time and enjoy our family." It got very quiet in the laundry room as the women continued sewing the pants. Suddenly, they realized that the first wife was patching the seat of the pants, and the other was patching the knees.

2. **The meek will be supplied by God.**
   PSALM 22:26
   26 *The meek shall eat and be satisfied: they shall praise the LORD that seek him: your heart shall live for ever*

   Quote—The axe cannot boast of the trees it has cut down. It could do nothing but for the woodsman. He made it, he sharpened it, he used it. The moment he throws it aside, it becomes only old iron. O that I may never lose sight of this.—Dr. Samuel Brengle

B. *Meekness Is Praised by Jesus*
   MATTHEW 5:5
   5 *Blessed are the meek: for they shall inherit the earth.*

   To trust Christ as Saviour requires meekness. One day those who have trusted Him will reign with Him.

   ISAIAH 29:19
   19 *The meek also shall increase their joy in the LORD, and the poor among men shall rejoice in the Holy One of Israel.*

II. The Operation of Meekness

The service of a Christian manifests itself in gentle spirit.

EPHESIANS 4:2
2 *With all lowliness and meekness, with longsuffering, forbearing one another in love;*

A. *Properly Responds in Difficulty*
   We cannot control the actions of others, but we can control our response to them by the power of the Spirit.

   TITUS 3:2
   2 *To speak evil of no man, to be no brawlers, but gentle, shewing all meekness unto all men.*

1 TIMOTHY 6:11

11 *But thou, O man of God, flee these things; and follow after righteousness, godliness, faith, love, patience, meekness.*

Gentleness diffuses a bad temper. Meekness is the strength to back away from a fight you could win.

Illustration—A missionary in Jamaica was once questioning some little boys on the meaning of Matthew 5:5 and asked, "Who are the meek?" A boy answered, "Those who give soft answers to rough questions." We shall do well to remember this child's definition. (pulpithelps.com)

B. *Properly Responds in Marriage*

Illustration—A man once said, "I married Miss Right. I just didn't know her first name was Always."

EPHESIANS 5:21

21 *Submitting yourselves one to another in the fear of God.*

1 PETER 3:1–4

1 *Likewise, ye wives, be in subjection to your own husbands; that, if any obey not the word, they also may without the word be won by the conversation of the wives;*
2 *While they behold your chaste conversation coupled with fear.*
3 *Whose adorning let it not be that outward adorning of plaiting the hair, and of wearing of gold, or of putting on of apparel;*
4 *But let it be the hidden man of the heart, in that which is not corruptible, even the ornament of a meek and quiet spirit, which is in the sight of God of great price.*

Quote—Meekness is the ability to disagree agreeably.

Illustration—First-grader Melanie had announced that she was engaged to marry the young gentleman next door, but the engagement was broken abruptly. "Why aren't you going to marry Danny?" asked Melanie's mother, with a twinkle in her eye. "Well," replied the child loftily, "he just isn't ready for marriage yet. And besides that, he scribbled in my coloring book."

C. *Properly Responds in Witnessing*
Christians cannot win spiritual battles in the flesh.

1 PETER 3:15–16
15 *But sanctify the Lord God in your hearts: and be ready always to give an answer to every man that asketh you a reason of the hope that is in you with meekness and fear:*
16 *Having a good conscience; that, whereas they speak evil of you, as of evildoers, they may be ashamed that falsely accuse your good conversation in Christ.*

III. The Opportunity of Meekness

A. *To Reveal Christ in You*
MATTHEW 11:29–30
29 *Take my yoke upon you, and learn of me; for I am meek and lowly in heart: and ye shall find rest unto your souls.*
30 *For my yoke is easy, and my burden is light.*

B. *To Reflect the Word of God*
JAMES 1:21–22
21 *Wherefore lay apart all filthiness and superfluity of naughtiness, and receive with meekness the engrafted word, which is able to save your souls.*
22 *But be ye doers of the word, and not hearers only, deceiving your own selves.*

1. **Meekness causes us to receive the Word.**
   A meek person is teachable. However, a person who cannot admit any mistakes in life will end up a lonely person.

2. **Meekness causes us to live the Word.**
   PHILIPPIANS 2:16
   16 Holding forth the word of life; that I may rejoice in the day of Christ, that I have not run in vain, neither laboured in vain.

Conclusion

Jesus is the ultimate example of meekness. When He endured the torment of Calvary, He still had all the power of His earthly ministry. He was still capable of raising the dead, healing the blind, and mending the hurting. He could have come down off the cross and destroyed the very soldiers who mocked Him. However, in meekness, He remained on the cross and endured physical torment and the sin of the entire human race. Christ's meekness was anything but weakness. It was supernatural strength.

If we are to show forth the spirit of Christ, we must put on meekness by His Spirit.

COLOSSIANS 3:12–13
12 Put on therefore, as the elect of God, holy and beloved, bowels of mercies, kindness, humbleness of mind, meekness, longsuffering;
13 Forbearing one another, and forgiving one another, if any man have a quarrel against any: even as Christ forgave you, so also do ye.

OUTLINE TWENTY-SIX

WALKING WITH TEMPERANCE
GALATIANS 5:22–23

22 *But the fruit of the Spirit is love, joy, peace, longsuffering, gentleness, goodness, faith,*
23 *Meekness, temperance: against such there is no law.*

Introduction

Many problems in life are related to a lack of self-control. Self-control is only possible when we are under the Spirit's control!

EPHESIANS 5:18
18 *And be not drunk with wine, wherein is excess; but be filled with the Spirit;*

Many people feel their lives are out of control. They are overwhelmed by pressures and circumstances.

PROVERBS 25:28
28 *He that hath no rule over his own spirit is like a city that is broken down, and without walls.*

Christians would be wise to seek the fullness of the Holy Spirit in order to possess the strength needed to develop self-control.

I. Temperance Explained

Temperance has two facets:

A. Discretion

Discretion is knowing when to do the right thing at the right time. This quality helps us to practice integrity at a crucial moment of choice.

Proverbs 3:21–23
21 *My son, let not them depart from thine eyes: keep sound wisdom and discretion:*
22 *So shall they be life unto thy soul, and grace to thy neck.*
23 *Then shalt thou walk in thy way safely, and thy foot shall not stumble.*

Titus 2:1–2
1 *But speak thou the things which become sound doctrine:*
2 *That the aged men be sober, grave, temperate, sound in faith, in charity, in patience.*

B. Discipline

Illustration—Successful athletes make choices to practice when no one else does.

1 Corinthians 9:25–27
25 *And every man that striveth for the mastery is temperate in all things. Now they do it to obtain a corruptible crown; but we an incorruptible.*
26 *I therefore so run, not as uncertainly; so fight I, not as one that beateth the air:*

27 *But I keep under my body, and bring it into subjection: lest that by any means, when I have preached to others, I myself should be a castaway.*

1 Corinthians 9:24

24 *Know ye not that they which run in a race run all, but one receiveth the prize? So run, that ye may obtain.*

Illustration—It takes discipline to raise children consistently.

Ephesians 6:4

4 *And, ye fathers, provoke not your children to wrath: but bring them up in the nurture and admonition of the Lord.*

Illustration—A Cambridge professor named Coleridge was once talking with a man who told him that he did not believe in giving little children any religious instruction whatsoever. His theory was that the child's mind should not be prejudiced in any direction, but when he came to years of discretion he should be permitted to choose his religious opinions for himself. Coleridge said nothing; but after a while he asked his visitor if he would like to see his garden. The man said he would, and Coleridge took him out into the garden, where only weeds were growing. The man looked at Coleridge in surprise, and said, "Why, this is not a garden! There is nothing but weeds here!" "Well, you see," answered Coleridge, "I did not wish to infringe upon the liberty of the garden in any way, I was just giving the garden a chance to express itself and to choose its own production."

As the Apostle Paul charged Timothy, he explained that it takes temperance to keep a church in the right direction.

2 Timothy 4:1–3

1 *I charge thee therefore before God, and the Lord Jesus Christ, who shall judge the quick and the dead at his appearing and his kingdom;*

2 *Preach the word; be instant in season, out of season; reprove, rebuke, exhort with all longsuffering and doctrine.*

3 *For the time will come when they will not endure sound doctrine; but after their own lusts shall they heap to themselves teachers, having itching ears;*

II. Temperance Experienced

A. *A Disciplined Physical Life*

1 Corinthians 9:27

27 *But I keep under my body, and bring it into subjection: lest that by any means, when I have preached to others, I myself should be a castaway.*

1. **The flesh fights the Spirit.**

   Galatians 5:16–17

   16 *This I say then, Walk in the Spirit, and ye shall not fulfil the lust of the flesh.*

   17 *For the flesh lusteth against the Spirit, and the Spirit against the flesh: and these are contrary the one to the other: so that ye cannot do the things that ye would.*

2. **The flesh is defeated through Calvary.**

   Romans 6:11–16

   11 *Likewise reckon ye also yourselves to be dead indeed unto sin, but alive unto God through Jesus Christ our Lord.*

   12 *Let not sin therefore reign in your mortal body, that ye should obey it in the lusts thereof.*

   13 *Neither yield ye your members as instruments of unrighteousness unto sin: but yield yourselves unto God, as those that are alive from the dead, and your members as instruments of righteousness unto God.*

   14 *For sin shall not have dominion over you: for ye are not under the law, but under grace.*

> 15 What then? shall we sin, because we are not under the law, but under grace? God forbid.
> 16 Know ye not, that to whom ye yield yourselves servants to obey, his servants ye are to whom ye obey; whether of sin unto death, or of obedience unto righteousness?

B. A Disciplined Thought Life
2 Corinthians 10:5

> 5 Casting down imaginations, and every high thing that exalteth itself against the knowledge of God, and bringing into captivity every thought to the obedience of Christ;

The word *imaginations* in Greek is *logismous*, meaning, "thoughts or fantasies against the truth of Christ or the revealed will of God."

III. Temperance Exemplified

How can we develop temperance going forward?

A. Admit Your Weakness
James 1:14–16

> 14 But every man is tempted, when he is drawn away of his own lust, and enticed.
> 15 Then when lust hath conceived, it bringeth forth sin: and sin, when it is finished, bringeth forth death.
> 16 Do not err, my beloved brethren.

B. Forget Your Past
Philippians 3:13–14

> 13 Brethren, I count not myself to have apprehended: but this one thing I do, forgetting those things which are behind, and reaching forth unto those things which are before,
> 14 I press toward the mark for the prize of the high calling of God in Christ Jesus.

Illustration—When children learn to walk, they fall many times. No one ever says about a child learning to walk, "Well he's just not meant to be a walker!"

C. Believe God Can Bring Change
Your beliefs control your behavior.

ROMANS 12:2

2 *And be not conformed to this world: but be ye transformed by the renewing of your mind, that ye may prove what is that good, and acceptable, and perfect, will of God.*

PHILIPPIANS 4:13

13 *I can do all things through Christ which strengtheneth me.*

D. Become Accountable
ECCLESIASTES 4:12

12 *And if one prevail against him, two shall withstand him; and a threefold cord is not quickly broken.*

E. Avoid Temptation
In our flesh, we like to take the path of least resistance.

Illustration—On the TV show "Hee Haw," Doc Campbell is confronted by a patient who says he broke his arm in two places. The doc replies, "Well then, stay out of them places!"

Quote—When you flee temptation, be sure you don't leave a forwarding address.—Unknown

EPHESIANS 4:26–27

26 *Be ye angry, and sin not: let not the sun go down upon your wrath:*
27 *Neither give place to the devil.*

Quote—If you don't want rotten apples, stay out of the devil's orchard.—Unknown

Quote—It is easier to suppress the first desire than to satisfy all that follow it.—Benjamin Franklin

Note—We should avoid the places and friends that are likely to draw us into temptation.

1 Corinthians 15:33
33 *Be not deceived: evil communications corrupt good manners.*

The word *communications* means "companionship." In other words, bad company corrupts good character.

F. Depend on God's Power

Galatians 5:16–17
16 *This I say then, Walk in the Spirit, and ye shall not fulfil the lust of the flesh.*
17 *For the flesh lusteth against the Spirit, and the Spirit against the flesh: and these are contrary the one to the other: so that ye cannot do the things that ye would.*

Walking in the Spirit consists of not only trying but also trusting!

Philippians 2:13
13 *For it is God which worketh in you both to will and to do of his good pleasure.*

Conclusion

The secret to self-control is Christ's control. By walking in the Spirit's control, we can experience temperance and exemplify it to those around us.

OUTLINE TWENTY-SEVEN

A Spiritual Life
Galatians 5:24–26

24 *And they that are Christ's have crucified the flesh with the affections and lusts.*
25 *If we live in the Spirit, let us also walk in the Spirit.*
26 *Let us not be desirous of vain glory, provoking one another, envying one another.*

Introduction

The spiritual life is not something we contrive, but it is something God gives.

Galatians 2:20
20 *I am crucified with Christ: nevertheless I live; yet not I, but Christ liveth in me: and the life which I now live in the flesh I live by the faith of the Son of God, who loved me, and gave himself for me.*

I. The Position of a Spiritual Christian (v. 24)

A. *A Statement of Ownership*

Verse 24 says, "They that are Christ's," meaning "they that belong to Christ."

1. **We are purchased by Christ.**

   1 Corinthians 6:19–20

   19 What? know ye not that your body is the temple of the Holy Ghost which is in you, which ye have of God, and ye are not your own?

   20 For ye are bought with a price: therefore glorify God in your body, and in your spirit, which are God's.

2. **We are in Christ.**

   2 Corinthians 5:17

   17 Therefore if any man be in Christ, he is a new creature: old things are passed away; behold, all things are become new.

   Ephesians 2:13

   13 But now in Christ Jesus ye who sometimes were far off are made nigh by the blood of Christ.

B. *A Statement of Position*

1. **A position of victory**

   Although former influences like the old man and the world still existed, they no longer dominated the Apostle Paul.

   Galatians 5:17

   17 For the flesh lusteth against the Spirit, and the Spirit against the flesh: and these are contrary the one to the other: so that ye cannot do the things that ye would.

2. A position of finality

Paul explains that everyone who belongs to Christ Jesus by faith in Him has crucified the flesh. Paul is saying that the flesh has been executed.

But how could that be in light of what he just said in this chapter about believers having a constant war with the ever-present flesh? This passage looks back to the cross, the time at which the death of the flesh was actually accomplished.

Illustration—Like a chicken with its head cut off, the flesh has been dealt a death blow, however it continues to flop around the barnyard of earth until the last nerve is stilled.

II. The Prompting of a Spiritual Christian (v. 25)

A. *He Lives in the Spirit*

GALATIANS 5:16

16 *This I say then, Walk in the Spirit, and ye shall not fulfil the lust of the flesh.*

ROMANS 8:10

10 *And if Christ be in you, the body is dead because of sin; but the Spirit is life because of righteousness.*

We are in the flesh geographically but not spiritually. Spiritually, we are "in Christ." This is our standing or position, and it does not change.

B. *He Is Led of the Spirit*

GALATIANS 5:18

18 *But if ye be led of the Spirit, ye are not under the law.*

If we are led by the Holy Spirit, then we don't need to be under the law because the Spirit will guide us in what is righteous, good, and true.

C. He Walks in the Spirit
1. A guided walk
JOHN 16:13–14

13 Howbeit when he, the Spirit of truth, is come, he will guide you into all truth: for he shall not speak of himself; but whatsoever he shall hear, that shall he speak: and he will shew you things to come.

14 He shall glorify me: for he shall receive of mine, and shall shew it unto you.

2. A worthy walk
COLOSSIANS 1:10

10 That ye might walk worthy of the Lord unto all pleasing, being fruitful in every good work, and increasing in the knowledge of God;

EPHESIANS 4:1–3

1 I therefore, the prisoner of the Lord, beseech you that ye walk worthy of the vocation wherewith ye are called,

2 With all lowliness and meekness, with longsuffering, forbearing one another in love;

3 Endeavouring to keep the unity of the Spirit in the bond of peace.

Quote—Watch out for any ministry or person who claims to be led by the Holy Spirit but acts contrary to the Word of God. And beware of any movement or group whose focus is the Holy Spirit. The Holy Spirit points not to Himself but to Jesus Christ.—George Sweeting

III. The Practice of a Spiritual Christian

Quote—When led of the Spirit, the child of God must be as ready to wait as to go, as prepared to be silent as to speak.—Lewis Sperry Chafer

A. Humble (v. 26a)

1 Corinthians 3:7

7 *So then neither is he that planteth any thing, neither he that watereth; but God that giveth the increase.*

James 4:16

16 *But now ye rejoice in your boastings: all such rejoicing is evil.*

1. Forgive one another.

Ephesians 4:32

32 *And be ye kind one to another, tenderhearted, forgiving one another, even as God for Christ's sake hath forgiven you.*

2. Rejoice for others.

Romans 12:15

15 *Rejoice with them that do rejoice, and weep with them that weep.*

3. Don't hold offenses.

Ephesians 4:31

31 *Let all bitterness, and wrath, and anger, and clamour, and evil speaking, be put away from you, with all malice:*

B. Helpful (v. 26b)

If we are not to be provoking one another, we should be helping one another.

James 3:14–16

14 *But if ye have bitter envying and strife in your hearts, glory not, and lie not against the truth.*

15 *This wisdom descendeth not from above, but is earthly, sensual, devilish.*

> 16 For where envying and strife is, there is confusion and every evil work.

C. Hopeful (v. 26c)

1 Corinthians 13:7–8

> 7 Beareth all things, believeth all things, hopeth all things, endureth all things.
> 8 Charity never faileth: but whether there be prophecies, they shall fail; whether there be tongues, they shall cease; whether there be knowledge, it shall vanish away.

Conclusion

Christians who walk in the Spirit will fulfill their responsibilities toward God and man. It is important for us to remember that if we walk in the flesh, we cannot and will not bear the fruit of the Spirit. When God's Spirit prompts our heart to move on His behalf or to rid ourselves of sin, we must not ignore Him.

1 Thessalonians 5:19

> 19 Quench not the Spirit.

OUTLINE TWENTY-EIGHT

A Restorative Church
Galatians 6:1

1   *Brethren, if a man be overtaken in a fault, ye which are spiritual, restore such an one in the spirit of meekness; considering thyself, lest thou also be tempted.*

Introduction

This passage of Scripture can help every Christian, every teacher, every home, and of course, every local church. Much of our week is spent helping to reconcile a lost world to Christ.

2 Corinthians 5:18
18   *And all things are of God, who hath reconciled us to himself by Jesus Christ, and hath given to us the ministry of reconciliation;*

But some of our time inevitably will be spent helping to restore other believers when they fall (not from salvation, but from fellowship).

The local church is a body of believers. It is not God's will that we sin, but He teaches us our proper response in times when church members fail.

The assumption of this passage is a repentant sinner. The church cannot restore an unrepentant sinner.

Luke 3:8

8   Bring forth therefore fruits worthy of repentance, and begin not to say within yourselves, We have Abraham to our father: for I say unto you, That God is able of these stones to raise up children unto Abraham.

I. The Reality of Failure

A. *The Affronts of Satan*

The word *overtaken* means "overwhelmed by or caught in."

Satan is always looking to bring harm to God's people by overwhelming them in temptation or catching them in a vice.

B. *The Aftermath of Temptation*

The word *fault* means "a lapse or deviation from the truth; a character flaw."

Hebrews 12:1

1   Wherefore seeing we also are compassed about with so great a cloud of witnesses, let us lay aside every weight, and the sin which doth so easily beset us, and let us run with patience the race that is set before us,

II. The Restoration of Forgiveness

A. *The Requirement*

1. Ye which are spiritual

We as Christians fall into one of two categories: we are either spiritual or carnal.

- The spiritual Christian is strong in the Lord.

Romans 15:1

1   We then that are strong ought to bear the infirmities of the weak, and not to please ourselves.

- The spiritual Christian is known by his fruit.

Galatians 5:22–23
22 *But the fruit of the Spirit is love, joy, peace, longsuffering, gentleness, goodness, faith,*
23 *Meekness, temperance: against such there is no law.*

2. **In a spirit of meekness**
1 Peter 3:15
15 *But sanctify the Lord God in your hearts: and be ready always to give an answer to every man that asketh you a reason of the hope that is in you with meekness and fear:*

1 Corinthians 10:12
12 *Wherefore let him that thinketh he standeth take heed lest he fall.*

Titus 3:2
2 *To speak evil of no man, to be no brawlers, but gentle, shewing all meekness unto all men.*

Illustration—Jesus restored Peter even after Peter had denied Him in a crucial moment (John 21).

It is not the church's place to bring chastisement upon a fallen Christian. Judgment is done only by God.

Quote—The Christian army is the only army in the world that shoots its wounded.—Unknown

Illustration—Jesus restored a woman who had fallen into adultery. There was no doubt that this woman was guilty because she was caught in the very act. However, Christ forgave her and restored her through his compassionate love.

JOHN 8:3–11

3 And the scribes and Pharisees brought unto him a woman taken in adultery; and when they had set her in the midst,

4 They say unto him, Master, this woman was taken in adultery, in the very act.

5 Now Moses in the law commanded us, that such should be stoned: but what sayest thou?

6 This they said, tempting him, that they might have to accuse him. But Jesus stooped down, and with his finger wrote on the ground, as though he heard them not.

7 So when they continued asking him, he lifted up himself, and said unto them, He that is without sin among you, let him first cast a stone at her.

8 And again he stooped down, and wrote on the ground.

9 And they which heard it, being convicted by their own conscience, went out one by one, beginning at the eldest, even unto the last: and Jesus was left alone, and the woman standing in the midst.

10 When Jesus had lifted up himself, and saw none but the woman, he said unto her, Woman, where are those thine accusers? hath no man condemned thee?

11 She said, No man, Lord. And Jesus said unto her, Neither do I condemn thee: go, and sin no more.

It is not our job as Christians to add more guilt to a sinner. Only the Holy Spirit can convict someone of sin. Our job is to love and restore.

However, sometimes in restoration there is a time someone may need to step down from a ministry or be placed off a team for a while. But the goal is to see fruit and to ultimately restore this person.

2 CORINTHIANS 2:7

7 So that contrariwise ye ought rather to forgive him, and comfort him, lest perhaps such a one should be swallowed up with overmuch sorrow.

B. **The Restoration**

The word *restore* means "to mend." This same word was used of James and John when they were mending their nets. The connotation of this word is that we should mend things with a fallen Christian so that he is useful once again.

ROMANS 15:1
1 We then that are strong ought to bear the infirmities of the weak, and not to please ourselves.

Illustration—A few years ago, a crazed man ran into a museum in Amsterdam and came to Rembrandt's painting *The Night Watch*. He took a knife and slashed it. A few months later a man entered St. Peter's Basilica in Rome. He took a hammer and smashed the *Pieta*. What did officials do? Did they throw the works away? No, they got the best artists of the day and paid a great price to have the works restored.

1. **Help the sinner recognize the sin.**

2. **Help restore the sinner to fellowship.**

   Illustration—Author and teacher Dr. Howard Hendricks tells the story of a young man who strayed from the Lord but was finally brought back by the help of a friend who really loved him. When there was full repentance and restoration, Dr. Hendricks asked this Christian how it felt to be away from the Lord. The young man said it seemed like he was out at sea, in deep water, deep trouble, and all his friends were on the shore hurling biblical accusations at him about justice, penalty, and wrong. "But, there was one Christian brother who actually swam out to get me and would not let me go. I fought him, but he pushed aside my fighting, grasped me, put a life jacket around me, and took me to shore. By the grace of God, he was the reason I was restored. He would not let me go."

Note—There is a difference between fellowship and ministry. Sometimes we can restore a fallen Christian to fellowship and even to ministry, but not to pastoral ministry.

1 Timothy 3:2
2 *A bishop then must be blameless, the husband of one wife, vigilant, sober, of good behaviour, given to hospitality, apt to teach;*

III. The Reasoning of the Faithful

A. Consideration

The word *consideration* is the Greek word *skopeo*, meaning, "to put the scope on yourself."

1 Timothy 4:16
16 *Take heed unto thyself, and unto the doctrine; continue in them: for in doing this thou shalt both save thyself, and them that hear thee.*

We must all continually be diligent to guard our own purity.

B. Caution: "Lest thou also be tempted"

Proverbs 16:18
18 *Pride goeth before destruction, and an haughty spirit before a fall.*

1 Corinthians 10:11–12
11 *Now all these things happened unto them for ensamples: and they are written for our admonition, upon whom the ends of the world are come.*
12 *Wherefore let him that thinketh he standeth take heed lest he fall.*

1 Corinthians 10:13
13 *There hath no temptation taken you but such as is common to man: but God is faithful, who will not suffer you to be*

tempted above that ye are able; but will with the temptation also make a way to escape, that ye may be able to bear it.

Conclusion

The reality is that we will all fail at one point in our Christian walk. While we walk in the Spirit, we also fight the flesh and its many temptations. Because of this, we should be quick to restore and forgive those who have fallen around us. We must love them and mend them so that they can once again be useful to the cause of Christ. And even in the process of restoring others, we must be cautious of our own personal walk with God, considering that we will also be tempted to sin.

OUTLINE TWENTY-NINE

Make Me a Blessing
Galatians 6:2–5

2 Bear ye one another's burdens, and so fulfil the law of Christ.
3 For if a man think himself to be something, when he is nothing, he deceiveth himself.
4 But let every man prove his own work, and then shall he have rejoicing in himself alone, and not in another.
5 For every man shall bear his own burden.

Introduction

Paul's challenge to the Galatian church thus far has been mixed with reproof and instruction. In this passage, the Apostle Paul continues to challenge these young believers in the way they treat each other. His instruction is relevant to the way we as Christians and members of local churches treat each other today.

The prayer of every believer's heart in response to the way he treats others should be threefold:

I. Make Me Helpful (v. 2)

The words *bear ye* are from the Greek word *bastazo*, meaning, "to take up in order to carry or bear, to put upon one's self (something) to be carried, to bear what is burdensome." This verb phrase is imperative, giving us a command, not an option.

A. In Love

JOHN 13:34

34 *A new commandment I give unto you, That ye love one another; as I have loved you, that ye also love one another.*

JOHN 15:12

12 *This is my commandment, That ye love one another, as I have loved you.*

B. In Labor

The word *burdens* in Greek is *baros*, meaning, "heaviness, weight, trouble." According to this passage, it is our duty to carry the heavy weights of other believers.

1 THESSALONIANS 5:14

14 *Now we exhort you, brethren, warn them that are unruly, comfort the feebleminded, support the weak, be patient toward all men.*

True love always labors despite difficult trials and burdens.

Quote—There are two times when a man doesn't understand a woman—before marriage and after marriage.

In light of the context of verse 1 in restoring the fallen brother, it would be logical in the context that the burden bearing is specifically referencing the realm of others' spiritual burdens and needs. This burden-bearing can carry over into physical needs as well.

Illustration—Years ago, the founder of Salvation Army, General William Booth, was on his death bed. The workers of the Salvation Army were gathered for their annual conference when they received a message from General Booth. The message simply read, "Others."

II. Make Me Humble (v. 3)

One of the dangers of bearing burdens is a know-it-all attitude. Sometimes when we are restoring and burden bearing we can begin to think too highly of ourselves.

A. *Beware of False Pride*

Illustration—The Reverend Walter Chellberg discovered the following two epitaphs in a local cemetery. "She lived with her husband fifty years and died in a confident hope of a better life." "Here lies Jane Smith, wife of Thomas Smith, marble cutter. This monument was erected by her husband as a tribute to her memory and as a specimen of his work. Monument of the same size: $350." (Reader's Digest, March 2007, p. 180)

B. *Beware of Self-Deception*

If you have a proud attitude, you will eventually say something or do something that will show your pride.

PROVERBS 4:23

23 *Keep thy heart with all diligence; for out of it are the issues of life.*

We are all just sinners saved by grace. Our service is not indispensable. Our tithe and talents are not indispensable. All of our service should be done as unto the Lord.

The spiritual man does not think he is something or that he is nothing—he simply doesn't compare!

III. Make Me Honorable (vv. 4–5)

A. As I Prove My Work (v. 4)

The word *prove* in Greek is *dokimazo*, meaning, "to test, examine, prove, scrutinize (to see whether a thing is genuine or not), as metals; to recognize as genuine after examination, to approve, deem worthy."

The metaphor the Apostle Paul gives here is the obligation Christ lays upon his followers to examine their own works—whether they are genuine and worthy—because every believer will bear the load of the work he has done for Christ.

2 Corinthians 13:5a

5 *Examine yourselves, whether ye be in the faith; prove your own selves.*

Romans 14:10

10 *But why dost thou judge thy brother? or why dost thou set at nought thy brother? for we shall all stand before the judgment seat of Christ.*

James 4:15–17

15 *For that ye ought to say, If the Lord will, we shall live, and do this, or that.*

16 *But now ye rejoice in your boastings: all such rejoicing is evil.*

17 *Therefore to him that knoweth to do good, and doeth it not, to him it is sin.*

B. As I Bear My Burdens (v. 5)

Some may question why verse 2 tells us to bear one another's burdens while verse 5 commands us to bear our own burdens. The answer is simple: Verse 2 is speaking of our service. Verse 5 is speaking of our personal responsibility.

Note—We are commanded to assume personal responsibility for our actions and works.

2 Thessalonians 3:10–11
10 For even when we were with you, this we commanded you, that if any would not work, neither should he eat.
11 For we hear that there are some which walk among you disorderly, working not at all, but are busybodies.

Illustration—The sign in the store window read: NO HELP WANTED. As two men passed by, one said to the other, "You should apply—you'd be great."

2 Thessalonians 3:12–13
12 Now them that are such we command and exhort by our Lord Jesus Christ, that with quietness they work, and eat their own bread.
13 But ye, brethren, be not weary in well doing.

A spiritual Christian is willing to be helpful, humble, and honorable in bearing other Christians' burdens, but he is also prepared to stand alone in carrying his responsibilities.

Conclusion

One way to detect your spiritual growth is by the way you handle burdens.

Do you see the burdens of others? Help them carry them.

Do you have burdens of your own? Take them to the Lord!

1 Peter 5:7
7 Casting all your care upon him; for he careth for you.

OUTLINE THIRTY

Sowing and Reaping
Galatians 6:6–8

6 Let him that is taught in the word communicate unto him that teacheth in all good things.
7 Be not deceived; God is not mocked: for whatsoever a man soweth, that shall he also reap.
8 For he that soweth to his flesh shall of the flesh reap corruption; but he that soweth to the Spirit shall of the Spirit reap life everlasting.

Introduction

This portion of Galatians centers on God's law of sowing and reaping. For those who are unfamiliar with the labors of sowing and the rewards of reaping, this can be a test of faith—until they do it. Regardless, if someone has been sowing for many years or is just beginning to contemplate this principle, their motivation for doing so will consist of one or all of these three:

I. Bond of Love (v. 6)

Sometimes a love for souls or the brethren causes Christians to invest their time or money. The example that Paul uses here is the love between the church and their pastor.

A. *From Those Who Are Taught*

1. **Taught the Word**

   HEBREWS 4:12

   12 For the word of God is quick, and powerful, and sharper than any twoedged sword, piercing even to the dividing asunder of soul and spirit, and of the joints and marrow, and is a discerner of the thoughts and intents of the heart.

   The word *taught* is the Greek word *katecheo*, meaning, "to sound towards, sound down upon, resound; to teach orally, to instruct, to inform by word of mouth, to be orally informed."

2. **Taught by pastors and teachers**

   EPHESIANS 4:11–12

   11 And he gave some, apostles; and some, prophets; and some, evangelists; and some, pastors and teachers.

   12 For the perfecting of the saints, for the work of the ministry, for the edifying of the body of Christ:

   2 TIMOTHY 4:2

   2 Preach the word; be instant in season, out of season; reprove, rebuke, exhort with all longsuffering and doctrine.

B. *To Those Who Teach*

The word *communicate* in Greek is *koinoneo*, meaning, "to come into communion or fellowship with, to become a sharer, be made a partner; to enter into fellowship, join one's self to an associate, make one's self a sharer or partner."

The congregation should communicate (share) with those who teach. Communication is expressed in two ways:

- By verbal communication back and forth. The communication here in the context of teacher to student, student to teacher.

- By giving of material goods to help someone out, in this case meeting the needs of the teacher—an expression of gratitude for what they are doing.

PHILIPPIANS 4:16–17
16 *For even in Thessalonica ye sent once and again unto my necessity.*
17 *Not because I desire a gift: but I desire fruit that may abound to your account.*

HEBREWS 13:16
16 *But to do good and to communicate forget not: for with such sacrifices God is well pleased.*

1 TIMOTHY 5:17
17 *Let the elders that rule well be counted worthy of double honour, especially they who labour in the word and doctrine.*

II. Bound by a Law (v. 7)

The law of sowing and reaping is an immutable, unalterable principle.

A. *Consider the Seed*

The kind of seed determines the harvest.

ROMANS 2:6–9
6 *Who will render to every man according to his deeds:*

> *7 To them who by patient continuance in well doing seek for glory and honour and immortality, eternal life:*
>
> *8 But unto them that are contentious, and do not obey the truth, but obey unrighteousness, indignation and wrath,*
>
> *9 Tribulation and anguish, upon every soul of man that doeth evil, of the Jew first, and also of the Gentile;*

Proverbs 11:18

> *18 The wicked worketh a deceitful work: but to him that soweth righteousness shall be a sure reward.*

B. *Consider the Harvest*

1. **It will be later in time.**

   One of Satan's deceptions is to get us to think when we have sowed the wrong things into our lives that we will not reap the consequences. However, consequences are always delayed—sometimes a short time, sometimes a long time.

   On the other hand, when we are sowing godliness into our lives we must remember that this harvest is also delayed. We must not grow weary of doing right.

2. **It will be greater in proportion.**

III. Based on a Lesson (v. 8)

A. *Sowing to the Flesh Produces Corruption*

Numbers 32:23

> *23 But if ye will not do so, behold, ye have sinned against the Lord: and be sure your sin will find you out.*

1. **Personally**
   - In your conversation

     Illustration—Mel Trotter, a man known for his drinking before his salvation and then founder of Brotherhood of Rescue Mission Superintendents, once went to a restaurant with a group of men. After Trotter ordered a carbonated water, someone inquired into why he would order carbonated instead of filtered. Trotter answered, "The Lord saved me and gave me a new heart, but because of alcohol, I'll have to wait for a new stomach."

ROMANS 6:13
13 *Neither yield ye your members as instruments of unrighteousness unto sin: but yield yourselves unto God, as those that are alive from the dead, and your members as instruments of righteousness unto God.*

- In your media

PROVERBS 22:8
8 *He that soweth iniquity shall reap vanity: and the rod of his anger shall fail.*

Illustration—Facebook and other social media can be edifying or self-glorifying and flesh satisfying.

2. **Corporately**
America is corrupting because the church is corrupting.

2 PETER 2:19–20
19 *While they promise them liberty, they themselves are the servants of corruption: for of whom a man is overcome, of the same is he brought in bondage.*
20 *For if after they have escaped the pollutions of the world through the knowledge of the Lord and Saviour Jesus Christ, they are again entangled therein, and overcome, the latter end is worse with them than the beginning.*

- Church music

EPHESIANS 5:19
19 *Speaking to yourselves in psalms and hymns and spiritual songs, singing and making melody in your heart to the Lord;*

The criteria for music selection in the church should not be personal likes or dislikes. It should be holiness.

- Church pulpit ministry

B. *Sowing to the Spirit Produces Life*
   Ephesians 5:11
   11 *And have no fellowship with the unfruitful works of darkness, but rather reprove them.*

   - In our witness

     Proverbs 11:30
     30 *The fruit of the righteous is a tree of life; and he that winneth souls is wise.*

   - In our giving

     2 Corinthians 9:6–7
     6 *But this I say, He which soweth sparingly shall reap also sparingly; and he which soweth bountifully shall reap also bountifully.*
     7 *Every man according as he purposeth in his heart, so let him give; not grudgingly, or of necessity: for God loveth a cheerful giver.*

Conclusion

We engage in sowing and reaping because of a bond of love for Christ and His people and because of the laws of harvest. We based our faithfulness on the lesson that pleasing the flesh brings destruction, but pleasing the Lord brings eternal reward.

OUTLINE THIRTY-ONE

LET US NOT BE WEARY
GALATIANS 6:9

9 *And let us not be weary in well doing: for in due season we shall reap, if we faint not.*

Introduction

Because the ministry involves spiritual warfare, we all can get burdened. However, well doing is easier in itself than ill doing. The danger of growing weary in well doing arises only from our own human nature opposing good or the outward hindrances we may meet with from a gainsaying and persecuting world.

I. A Biblical Challenge—Do Not Grow Weary

2 THESSALONIANS 3:13
13 *But ye, brethren, be not weary in well doing.*

Satan does not want us involved in well doing.

Romans 2:6–7
6 *Who will render to every man according to his deeds:*
7 *To them who by patient continuance in well doing seek for glory and honour and immortality, eternal life:*

Quote—The Puritan saint John Brown wrote, "Many Christians are like children; they would sow and reap the same day."

It is easy to become tired of sowing and be anxious for the harvest.

Illustration—A man stopped to watch a little league baseball game. He asked one of the youngsters what the score was. "We're losing 18-0," was the answer. "Well," said the man, "I must say you don't look discouraged."

"Discouraged?" the boy said, puzzled. "Why should we be discouraged? We haven't come to bat yet."

A. Weariness Develops over Time

The phrase "grow weary" speaks of exhaustion and losing heart.

God is exhorting us not to let our lives get to the point of spiritual exhaustion. We are in danger of becoming exhausted when we are not keeping our walk with God fresh each day in the Word of God and in prayer.

Mark 1:35
35 *And in the morning, rising up a great while before day, he went out, and departed into a solitary place, and there prayed.*

Jesus was busy, but He balanced His life with personal time and communion with the Father.

1 Peter 3:17
17 *For it is better, if the will of God be so, that ye suffer for well doing, than for evil doing.*

B. Weariness Depletes the Spirit

This phrase is exhorting us not to get to the point of exhaustion or losing heart. Exhaustion and losing heart go together because the spirit is affected by physical exhaustion. Yet the inner man can be strengthened daily even when the body is tired.

2 Corinthians 4:16

16 *For which cause we faint not; but though our outward man perish, yet the inward man is renewed day by day.*

1. **We must consider Christ.**
   Hebrews 12:1–3
   1 *Wherefore seeing we also are compassed about with so great a cloud of witnesses, let us lay aside every weight, and the sin which doth so easily beset us, and let us run with patience the race that is set before us,*
   2 *Looking unto Jesus the author and finisher of our faith; who for the joy that was set before him endured the cross, despising the shame, and is set down at the right hand of the throne of God.*
   3 *For consider him that endured such contradiction of sinners against himself, lest ye be wearied and faint in your minds.*

2. **We must continue on.**
   We must determine to be patient in the Lord.

   Illustration—We live in a hurried society. If an Internet page takes more than eight seconds to load, the site will lose about a third of their visitors.

   1 Corinthians 15:58
   58 *Therefore, my beloved brethren, be ye stedfast, unmoveable, always abounding in the work of the Lord, forasmuch as ye know that your labour is not in vain in the Lord.*

Quote—A vision that is not worthy of sacrifice is not a Christlike vision.—Unknown

II. A Basic Reminder—Ye Shall Reap

JAMES 5:7–8

7 *Be patient therefore, brethren, unto the coming of the Lord. Behold, the husbandman waiteth for the precious fruit of the earth, and hath long patience for it, until he receive the early and latter rain.*
8 *Be ye also patient; stablish your hearts: for the coming of the Lord draweth nigh.*

A. *We Shall Reap Spiritual Growth*

JAMES 1:3–4

3 *Knowing this, that the trying of your faith worketh patience.*
4 *But let patience have her perfect work, that ye may be perfect and entire, wanting nothing.*

Quote—Many Christians spend six days a week sowing wild oats and then come to church and pray for crop failure.

B. *We Shall Reap Spiritual Rewards*

2 TIMOTHY 4:7–8

7 *I have fought a good fight, I have finished my course, I have kept the faith:*
8 *Henceforth there is laid up for me a crown of righteousness, which the Lord, the righteous judge, shall give me at that day: and not to me only, but unto all them also that love his appearing.*

C. *We Shall Reap Souls of Men*

PROVERBS 11:30

30 *The fruit of the righteous is a tree of life; and he that winneth souls is wise.*

Illustration—Some of the greatest missionaries of history devotedly spread the seed of God's Word and yet had to wait long periods before seeing the fruit of their efforts. William Carey, for example, labored seven years before the first Hindu convert was brought to Christ in India, and Adoniram Judson toiled seven years before his faithful preaching in Burma was rewarded.

III. A Binding Condition—If We Faint Not

A. *We Must Not Faint in the End*
The word faint means "to let up in the end."

2 CORINTHIANS 4:1
1 *Therefore seeing we have this ministry, as we have received mercy, we faint not;*

Illustration—Gideon was faint, yet he pursued when fighting the Midianites.

JUDGES 8:4
4 *And Gideon came to Jordan, and passed over, he, and the three hundred men that were with him, faint, yet pursuing them.*

B. *We Must Not Forget the Eternal*
2 CORINTHIANS 4:15–18
15 *For all things are for your sakes, that the abundant grace might through the thanksgiving of many redound to the glory of God.*
16 *For which cause we faint not; but though our outward man perish, yet the inward man is renewed day by day.*
17 *For our light affliction, which is but for a moment, worketh for us a far more exceeding and eternal weight of glory;*
18 *While we look not at the things which are seen, but at the things which are not seen: for the things which are seen are temporal; but the things which are not seen are eternal.*

1. **Souls are eternal.**
   MARK 8:36–37
   36 *For what shall it profit a man, if he shall gain the whole world, and lose his own soul?*
   37 *Or what shall a man give in exchange for his soul?*

2. **Stewardship is eternal.**
   MATTHEW 6:19–21
   19 *Lay not up for yourselves treasures upon earth, where moth and rust doth corrupt, and where thieves break through and steal:*
   20 *But lay up for yourselves treasures in heaven, where neither moth nor rust doth corrupt, and where thieves do not break through nor steal:*
   21 *For where your treasure is, there will your heart be also.*

   Quote—The world asks, "What does a man own?" Christ asks, "How does he use it?"—Andrew Murray

3. **Scriptures are eternal.**
   1 PETER 1:23–25
   23 *Being born again, not of corruptible seed, but of incorruptible, by the word of God, which liveth and abideth for ever.*
   24 *For all flesh is as grass, and all the glory of man as the flower of grass. The grass withereth, and the flower thereof falleth away:*
   25 *But the word of the Lord endureth for ever. And this is the word which by the gospel is preached unto you.*

C. *We Must Have Faith for the Future*
2 CORINTHIANS 5:7
7 *(For we walk by faith, not by sight:)*

Quote—Faith draws the poison from every grief, takes the sting from every loss, and quenches the fire of every pain.
—J. G. Holland

Quote—The beginning of anxiety is the end of faith, and the beginning of true faith is the end of anxiety.—George Müller

Quote—Sorrow looks back. Worry looks around. Faith looks up.—Unknown

Illustration—Florence Chadwick was the first woman to swim the English Channel in both directions. On the Fourth of July in 1951, she attempted to swim from Catalina Island to the California coast. The challenge was not so much the distance but the bone-chilling waters of the Pacific. To complicate matters, a dense fog lay over the entire area, making it impossible for her to see land. After about fifteen hours in the water, and within a half mile of her goal, Chadwick gave up. Later she told a reporter, "Look, I'm not excusing myself. But if I could have seen land, I might have made it." Not long afterward she attempted the feat again. This time she succeeded. (sermoncentral.com)

Conclusion

We have all experienced physical weariness in our lives at some point. However, the Bible commands us to not become weary in the work of the Lord. If we have our hope in Christ and daily refresh our faith through Him, we will gain the strength necessary to continue serving God and others.

Isaiah 40:30–31

30 *Even the youths shall faint and be weary, and the young men shall utterly fall:*

31 *But they that wait upon the Lord shall renew their strength; they shall mount up with wings as eagles; they shall run, and not be weary; and they shall walk, and not faint.*

OUTLINE THIRTY-TWO

GLORY IN THE CROSS
GALATIANS 6:11–15

11 *Ye see how large a letter I have written unto you with mine own hand.*
12 *As many as desire to make a fair shew in the flesh, they constrain you to be circumcised; only lest they should suffer persecution for the cross of Christ.*
13 *For neither they themselves who are circumcised keep the law; but desire to have you circumcised, that they may glory in your flesh.*
14 *But God forbid that I should glory, save in the cross of our Lord Jesus Christ, by whom the world is crucified unto me, and I unto the world.*
15 *For in Christ Jesus neither circumcision availeth any thing, nor uncircumcision, but a new creature.*

Introduction

This epistle to the Galatians was important to Paul. In fact, it was so important that he hand wrote it. In Galatians 4:15, Paul mentions that the Galatians would be willing to give him their eyes, indicating he had some kind of eye problem. In this current passage, Paul is plainly saying, "This is a long letter for me to write because writing is tough on my eyes, but I am taking the time out to do it so you can see how concerned I am for you."

Paul then proceeds to give the Galatians some encouragement through the message of the gospel.

I. The Realm of Their Trials (vv. 12–13)

A. *The Judaizers Were Shunning Persecution (v. 12).*

1. **They wanted recognition before men.**
   The phrase *make a fair shew* is from the Greek word *euprosopeo*, meaning, "to make a fair show; to please." These Judaizers were wanting to make a good impression with men.

   Just like the Judaizers, there are always those who for pride's sake want the attention and preeminence over others.

   3 John 9–10
   9 *I wrote unto the church: but Diotrephes, who loveth to have the preeminence among them, receiveth us not.*
   10 *Wherefore, if I come, I will remember his deeds which he doeth, prating against us with malicious words: and not content therewith, neither doth he himself receive the brethren, and forbiddeth them that would, and casteth them out of the church.*

2. **They wanted no recognition with the cross.**
   Quote—It is not from any true love for the cause of religion. It is, that they may avoid persecution from the Jews.—Albert Barnes

   Quote—They escaped the Jews' bitterness against Christianity, and the offence of Christ's cross, by making the Mosaic law a necessary preliminary; in fact, making

Christian converts into Jewish proselytes.—Jamieson, Fawcett, and Brown

The bottom line is that these Judaizers wanted no part of the persecution that went with the cross of Christ.

B. The Judaizers Were Seeking Self Glory (v. 13).

1. **Keeping the law was a vain goal.**
   Paul again reminds the Galatian believers that these Judaizers' teaching of circumcision and the keeping of the law for salvation was something they could never keep themselves.

2. **Outward glory was a vain goal.**
   Outward change (such as circumcision) can cause people to glory in the flesh. Inward change brought about by the work of the Holy Spirit can only glorify God.

   1 CORINTHIANS 1:31
   31 *That, according as it is written, He that glorieth, let him glory in the Lord.*

   2 CORINTHIANS 10:17–18
   17 *But he that glorieth, let him glory in the Lord.*
   18 *For not he that commendeth himself is approved, but whom the Lord commendeth.*

II. The Reason for Our Praise (v. 14)

A. We Glory in the Cross (v. 14 a)
The "glory" of the Judaizers was vain glory. Paul uses this same word when he says, "God forbid, that I should glory." Paul says there is nothing that a man can glory in except one thing—"save in the cross of our Lord Jesus Christ."

B. We Have Victory in the Cross (v. 14 b)

1. The cross is the symbol of victory.

JOHN 3:14–15

14 And as Moses lifted up the serpent in the wilderness, even so must the Son of man be lifted up:

15 That whosoever believeth in him should not perish, but have eternal life.

JOHN 8:28

28 Then said Jesus unto them, When ye have lifted up the Son of man, then shall ye know that I am he, and that I do nothing of myself; but as my Father hath taught me, I speak these things.

Jesus was crucified in the past to pay for our sins and satisfy the just demands of God's holiness by the shedding of His blood. The cross is the reminder of the payment and awful price Jesus paid with His own life.

2. The cross is the instrument of separation.

Paul concludes verse 14 by saying, "by whom the world is crucified unto me, and I unto the world," implying that because we claim the cross for salvation, we must be separate from the world.

Quote—There are no crown-wearers in heaven who were not cross-bearers here below.—C.H. Spurgeon

The believer is crucified with Christ not only at salvation but also in the present.

GALATIANS 2:20

20 I am crucified with Christ: nevertheless I live; yet not I, but Christ liveth in me: and the life which I now live in the flesh I live by the faith of the Son of God, who loved me, and gave himself for me.

The verb "is crucified" is in the perfect tense, allowing the Galatians to see that it has already happened in the past but is still affective in their lives now in the present.

III. The Result of Salvation (v. 15)

A. Salvation Is Not Evidenced in Mandated Works (v. 15a)

The word *availeth* in Greek is *ischuo*, meaning, "to be strong, to have power, to have power as shown by extraordinary deeds; to be a force." In Christ Jesus nothing has any force or influence to salvation. Neither following the law nor living without the law gives any advantage to the sinner.

When a sinner is born again, it does not matter whether he was physically altered by circumcision or not. Circumcision does not place any person into a position of greater prominence nor does it lower him if he is uncircumcised. The Judaizers taught otherwise, thus their message was one of legalism.

Strictly defined, legalism is adding works to salvation—attempting to mix human works with God's grace. Legalism in this sense is firmly rebutted all throughout the epistle of Galatians. There is, however, a sense in which we can become legalistic in our spirit by focusing on performance rather than elevating God's grace. This form of legalistic thinking is also seen throughout the New Testament. For example, Jesus warned about the "tradition of the elders"—man-made rules that in some instances actually contradicted the law of God, and in other instances added to God's law.

MATTHEW 15:1–8

1 *Then came to Jesus scribes and Pharisees, which were of Jerusalem, saying,*
2 *Why do thy disciples transgress the tradition of the elders? for they wash not their hands when they eat bread.*

> 3 But he answered and said unto them, Why do ye also transgress the commandment of God by your tradition?
> 4 For God commanded, saying, Honour thy father and mother: and, He that curseth father or mother, let him die the death.
> 5 But ye say, Whosoever shall say to his father or his mother, It is a gift, by whatsoever thou mightest be profited by me;
> 6 And honour not his father or his mother, he shall be free. Thus have ye made the commandment of God of none effect by your tradition.
> 7 Ye hypocrites, well did Esaias prophesy of you, saying,
> 8 This people draweth nigh unto me with their mouth, and honoureth me with their lips; but their heart is far from me.

Jesus also rebuked the Pharisees for adding extrabiblical rules that became burdensome and unhealthy.

Matthew 23:4
> 4 For they bind heavy burdens and grievous to be borne, and lay them on men's shoulders; but they themselves will not move them with one of their fingers.

Even as we shun doctrinal legalism, we must be careful to avoid what could be called "practical legalism" as well.

B. Salvation Is Evidenced in a Changed Life (v.15b)

The only force that can have any influence is the regenerated person who now has received the new nature through the Spirit.

2 Corinthians 5:17
> 17 Therefore if any man be in Christ, he is a new creature: old things are passed away; behold, all things are become new.

The warning is to saved men about the dangers of bragging about the outward conformities or religious rituals that the Judaizers were promoting. These religious rituals place the believer into a legalistic system that teaches that outward conformity will bring full acceptance before God. This belief system negates the acceptance that is found only in Christ Jesus through salvation, for nothing else needs to be added to salvation for us to be accepted by God.

EPHESIANS 1:6–8
6 *To the praise of the glory of his grace, wherein he hath made us accepted in the beloved.*
7 *In whom we have redemption through his blood, the forgiveness of sins, according to the riches of his grace;*
8 *Wherein he hath abounded toward us in all wisdom and prudence;*

Conclusion

When Christ carried His cross to Golgotha, he carried a weight that only He could bear. As He was crucified, he bore the weight of the sins of the whole world upon His shoulders. Through His perfect sacrifice, we know forgiveness and will soon know eternal life. Our feeble works cannot compare to His sacrifice. And nothing we do could make His sacrifice more perfect. Truly, we glory not in our works but only in His cross.

OUTLINE THIRTY-THREE

Paul's Closing
Galatians 6:16–18

16 And as many as walk according to this rule, peace be on them, and mercy, and upon the Israel of God.

17 From henceforth let no man trouble me: for I bear in my body the marks of the Lord Jesus.

18 Brethren, the grace of our Lord Jesus Christ be with your spirit. Amen.

Introduction

As Paul concludes this letter, he not only expresses the grace of God in his spirit toward the Galatian believers but also closes with the final reminder about God's wonderful grace.

Paul emphasizes three imperatives in the closing of his letter to the Galatians:

I. The Pre-requisite for Peace (v. 16)

A. A Walk of Peace

Paul begins verse 16 by saying, "And as many as walk according to this rule, peace be on them."

The word *walk* in Greek is *stoicheo*, meaning, "to proceed in a row, go in order." This same word is used throughout the New Testament referring to walking in relation to others and to an orderly life.

Paul addresses those who are walking in accordance to the order set in the gospel, those who have not followed the Judaizers.

PHILIPPIANS 3:16–17
16 *Nevertheless, whereto we have already attained, let us walk by the same rule, let us mind the same thing.*
17 *Brethren, be followers together of me, and mark them which walk so as ye have us for an ensample.*

COLOSSIANS 2:6–7
6 *As ye have therefore received Christ Jesus the Lord, so walk ye in him:*
7 *Rooted and built up in him, and stablished in the faith, as ye have been taught, abounding therein with thanksgiving.*

B. A Walk of Order

1. **By a rule—"according to this rule"**
   The word *rule* in Greek is *kanon*, meaning, "from kane (a straight reed, e.g. rod); a measuring rod; any rule or standard, a principle for judging, living, acting."

   This rule by which Paul wants the Galatian Christians to live is twofold:

   - According to the gospel given them

   GALATIANS 1:10
   10 *For do I now persuade men, or God? or do I seek to please men? for if I yet pleased men, I should not be the servant of Christ.*

- According to glorying in the cross

GALATIANS 6:14

14 But God forbid that I should glory, save in the cross of our Lord Jesus Christ, by whom the world is crucified unto me, and I unto the world.

Illustration—English evangelist George Whitefield (1714–1770) learned that it was more important to please God than to please men. Knowing that he was doing what was honoring to the Lord kept him from discouragement when he was falsely accused by his enemies. At one point in his ministry, Whitefield received a vicious letter accusing him of wrongdoing. His reply was brief and courteous: "I thank you heartily for your letter. As for what you and my other enemies are saying against me, I know worse things about myself than you will ever say about me. With love in Christ, George Whitefield."

2. **With God's reward**

Peace and mercy could only come by the way of the cross, not through man's efforts to keep the law or live by good works.

ROMANS 5:1

1 Therefore being justified by faith, we have peace with God through our Lord Jesus Christ:

Quote—Jesus is no security against life's storms, but He is perfect security in them.—Unknown

Paul closes verse 16 by wishing a blessing "upon the Israel of God." This blessing was especially intended to all the saved Jews teaching salvation by grace apart from circumcision. This was the same doctrinal conclusion reached by the Jerusalem council in Acts 15.

II. The Plea of the Apostle (v. 17)

A. *An Immediate Plea*

The word *henceforth* means, "hereafter, for the future."

The phrase *let no man trouble* in Greek is *parecho*, meaning "to bring one something either favorable or unfavorable."

This letter to the Galatians is now the point of reference concerning Paul's official position for all future questions that might arise. They do not need to ask him about it again.

B. *An Earned Plea*

The reason Paul could make this plea is that he bore the literal scars and marks he had received for preaching the gospel of Christ and suffered at the hands of the Jews as well as the Gentiles.

> 2 CORINTHIANS 11:23–28
> 23 *Are they ministers of Christ? (I speak as a fool) I am more; in labours more abundant, in stripes above measure, in prisons more frequent, in deaths oft.*
> 24 *Of the Jews five times received I forty stripes save one.*
> 25 *Thrice was I beaten with rods, once was I stoned, thrice I suffered shipwreck, a night and a day I have been in the deep;*
> 26 *In journeyings often, in perils of waters, in perils of robbers, in perils by mine own countrymen, in perils by the heathen, in perils in the city, in perils in the wilderness, in perils in the sea, in perils among false brethren;*
> 27 *In weariness and painfulness, in watchings often, in hunger and thirst, in fastings often, in cold and nakedness.*
> 28 *Beside those things that are without, that which cometh upon me daily, the care of all the churches.*

Illustration—On a wall in Charles Spurgeon's bedroom, he had a plaque with Isaiah 48:10 on it: "I have chosen thee in the furnace of affliction." "It is no mean thing to be chosen of God," he wrote. "God's choice makes chosen men choice men.... We are chosen, not in the palace, but in the furnace. In the furnace, beauty is marred, fashion is destroyed, strength is melted, glory is consumed; yet here eternal love reveals its secrets, and declares its choice."

III. The Prayer for the People (v. 18)

A. Grace from Christ

The grace from our Lord Jesus is also seen clearly in 2 Corinthians 8:9.

2 Corinthians 8:9

9 *For ye know the grace of our Lord Jesus Christ, that, though he was rich, yet for your sakes he became poor, that ye through his poverty might be rich.*

Even in Paul's closing, he reminds the Galatians that salvation is all of grace with no works necessary.

Quote—Thou Son of the Blessed, what grace was manifest in Thy condescension! Grace brought Thee down from heaven; Grace stripped Thee of Thy glory; Grace made Thee poor and despicable; Grace made Thee bear such burdens of sin, such burdens of sorrow, such burdens of God's curse as are unspeakable.—John Bunyan

B. Grace upon You

Paul asks that the same grace that Christ saved them with also be with their spirit. The spirit is in reference to the human spirit which is regenerated by the Holy Spirit.

John 3:3

3 *Jesus answered and said unto him, Verily, verily, I say unto thee, Except a man be born again, he cannot see the kingdom of God.*

Conclusion

As the Apostle Paul closes his letter to the Galatians, he reminds them once again of the grace by which they were saved, thereby bringing his letter full circle. It is as if he wants to remind the Galatians that the grace of God was sufficient for them in times past without the works of the law, and it is also sufficient for them in the present.

For us as believers, we can also be assured that God's saving grace that changed our lives will forever be sufficient for living grace as well. It is our responsibility now to share this message with a searching world.

APPENDIX

Additional Resources for Study

Greene, Oliver B. *The Epistle of Paul the Apostle to the Galatians.* Greenville, South Carolina: The Gospel Hour Inc. 1962

Ironside, H.A. *Galatians Ephesians (In The Heavenlies).* Neptune, New Jersey: Loizeaux Brothers Inc. 1981

Jamieson, Robert, A. R. Fausset, and David Brown. *A Commentary, Critical, Experimental, and Practical, on the Old and New Testaments.* Glasgow: William Collins, 1871.

MacArthur. John F. *The MacArthur New Testament Commentary, Galations.* The Moody Bible Institute of Chicago. 1987

Pfeiffer, Charles F., and Everett F. Harrison. *The Wycliffe Bible Commentary.* Chicago: Moody, 1962.

Phillips, John. *Exploring Galatians: An Expository Commentary.* Grand Rapids, Michigan: Kregel Publications. 2004

Wiersbe, Warren W. *Wiersbe's Expository Outlines on the Old Testament.* Wheaton, IL: Victor, 1993.

* Many of these resources, as well as other Bible study tools, can also be accessed online through helpful resource websites. The following websites may assist you in further study of Galatians:

Blue Letter Bible. http://www.blueletterbible.org/.

BibleApps.com: Online Bible for the Mobile Web. http://bibleapps.com.

Bible Suite: Online Bible, Concordance, Topical, Strong's, Greek and Hebrew. http://www.biblesuite.com/.

Bible Study Tools Online—Verses, Commentaries, Concordances, Verses, Parallel Versions. http://www.biblestudytools.com.

Also available from
Striving Together Publications

Philippians
Designed as a practical study help to pastors, teachers, and any Christian who desires to study God's Word, these expanded outlines from Paul Chappell walk verse by verse through the book of Philippians. These are perfect for sermon preparation or personal Bible study. (200 pages, hardback)

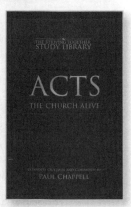

Acts
This volume contains over 500 pages of expanded outlines and comments that cover every verse in the book of Acts. Thousands of hours in preparation, these pages will give you a strong foundational understanding of the first-century church. Each of the eighty-two studies brings practical application to the local church and to your Christian life. (544 pages, hardback)

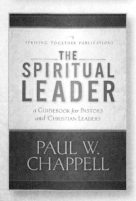

The Spiritual Leader
The Spiritual Leader summarizes a biblical philosophy of spiritual leadership that has been lived out dynamically through the life of the author. Every principle in these chapters flows from the Word of God and from a heart that has effectively served God's people for over two decades. Every page will challenge you to serve more effectively and to lead with greater understanding and passion. (336 pages, hardback)

strivingtogether.com

Visit us online

strivingtogether.com

wcbc.edu